1995

The Investor's Self-Teaching Seminars

INVESTING IN HIGH-YIELD STOCKS

AF855100

TPM

The Investor's Self-Teaching Seminars

INVESTING IN HIGH-YIELD STOCKS

One of a Series of Hands-On Workshops Dedicated to the Serious Investor

Peter D. Heerwagen

Probus Publishing Company
Chicago, Illinois

© 1989 Peter D. Heerwagen

ALL RIGHTS RESERVED. No part of this publication may be reproduced, stored in a retrieval system, or transmitted by any means, electronic, mechanical, photocopying, recording or otherwise, without the prior written permission of the publisher and the copyright holder.

This publication is designed to provide accurate and authoritative information in regard to the subject matter covered. It is sold with the understanding that the publisher is not engaged in rendering legal, accounting or other professional service.

FROM A DECLARATION OF PRINCIPLES JOINTLY ADOPTED BY A COMMITTEE OF THE AMERICAN BAR ASSOCIATION AND A COMMITTEE OF PUBLISHERS.

Library of Congress Cataloging-in-Publication Data Available

ISBN 1-55738-055-4

Printed in the United States of America

1 2 3 4 5 6 7 8 9 0

CONTENTS

Preface

This self-teaching seminar book will show you how to analyze high-yield stocks for your investment portfolio. You will also learn how to select stocks with good dividend growth prospects, for not only is it beneficial to receive generous income up front, but it's also rewarding to cash in on increasing returns over the years. Rising dividends pave the way for higher stock prices.

Purchasing high-yield stocks is part of a defensive investment strategy designed to cope with today's volatile markets. It's used by investors with moderate to low risk tolerance who want portfolio exposure to the greater long-term benefits offered by equity investing. The current yield provides downside protection for stock prices during market declines, while increasing dividends translate into capital appreciation. And high-yielding equity investments are more attractive than ever before due to recent changes in the federal income tax laws.

In the aftermath of the 1987 stock market crash many investors retreated to the safe haven of the bond market or parked funds in bank CDs or money market funds. They want reduced volatility and assured income for their investment portfolios. Yet it may be a mistake to place too much emphasis on fixed-income securities when an attractive alternative is available—the high-yield stock.

Often referred to as bond substitutes because of their excellent current income, relatively stable prices, and sensitivity to interest rates, high-yield stocks offer the added benefits of an increasing stream of income and the possibility of capital appreciation. These are stocks of established companies with long histories of dividend payments to their shareholders.

The high-yield stock investment strategy is appropriate for a variety of investors. Those wanting to minimize the risks of equity investing are certainly one group that's grown rapidly since the October, 1987 stock market debacle. Owners of small pension plans are also candidates for high-yield stocks. Through the magic of compounding of dividend income in a tax-deferred environment, these accounts can grow quickly. Retired persons with personal investment funds are a third group of investors who stand to benefit from the high-yield strategy, for increasing dividends goes a long ways toward offsetting the ravages of inflation on their fixed incomes.

This book will show you how to invest in high-yielding stocks which are reasonably valued and have good dividend growth possibilities leading to higher share prices down the road. Successful implementation of this strategy requires a willingness to avoid the temptation of investing in current market fads in the search of quick profits. It calls for a long-term philosophy where the greatest returns go to the patient investor.

Chapter One

INTRODUCTION

Despite the run-up in stock prices in recent years, over one-half of the total return from equity investments during that time was accounted for by cash dividends. That's right, more than 50 percent. Furthermore, for the past 30 years, more than two-thirds of the growth of capital from investing in the Standard & Poor's 500 Composite Stock Index (the S&P 500) came from both dividend income and the compounding of reinvested dividend income. This amply illustrates the powerful impact of dividends on investment success. Experienced high-yield stock investors are already aware of this phenomenon. Readers of this self-teaching seminar book will learn more about the magic of dividend income in the pages that follow.

Exhibit 1 shows the annual income return and capital appreciation return (depreciation in some years) for the S&P 500 during the 1978-1987 period. When added together, these two return components measure total return. As can be seen, dividend income is clearly a more stable and predictable source of investment return than capital appreciation. It fluctuated between +4 percent and +6 percent, while the capital return component varied from −10 percent to +27 percent. Dividend stability is an important phenomenon because it's one of the major benefits for high-yield stock investors.

Not only does the yield provide more stability to the total return equation, but there is also an increasing dollar return over time, as dividends increase and are reinvested. Yields may fluctuate from year to year, but the total dollars per share paid out to stockholders increases every year. This is the beauty of rising dividends and the magic of compounding working together to benefit the high-yield stock investor.

Exhibit 1
Income Return VS. Capital Return*,
1978 — 1987

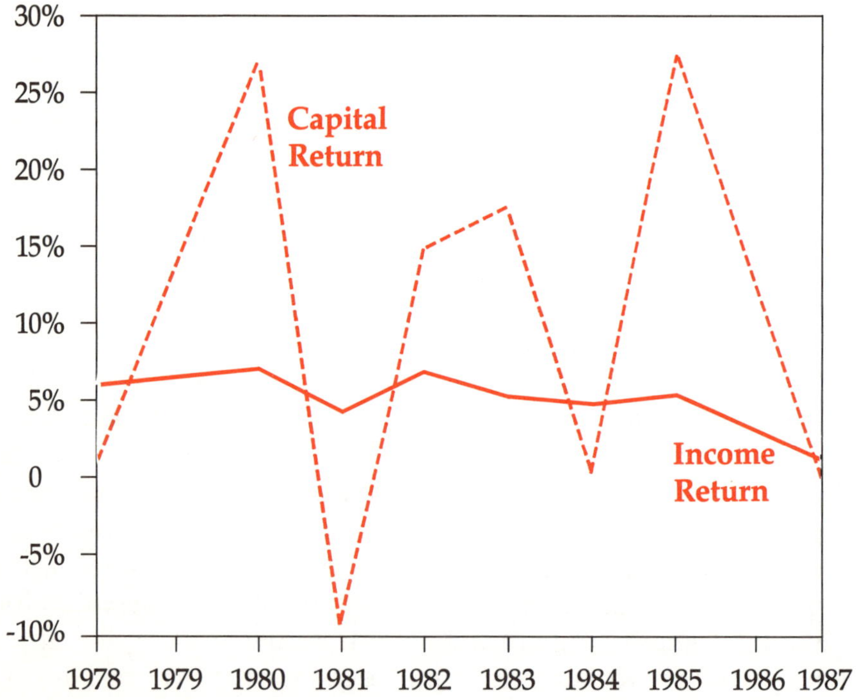

*Based on Standard & Poor's 500 Index from January 1, 1978, to December 31, 1987.

Source: *Stocks, Bonds, Bills and Inflation: 1988 Yearbook* Ibbotson Associates, Inc.

Exhibit 2
Rising Dividends —
S&P 500

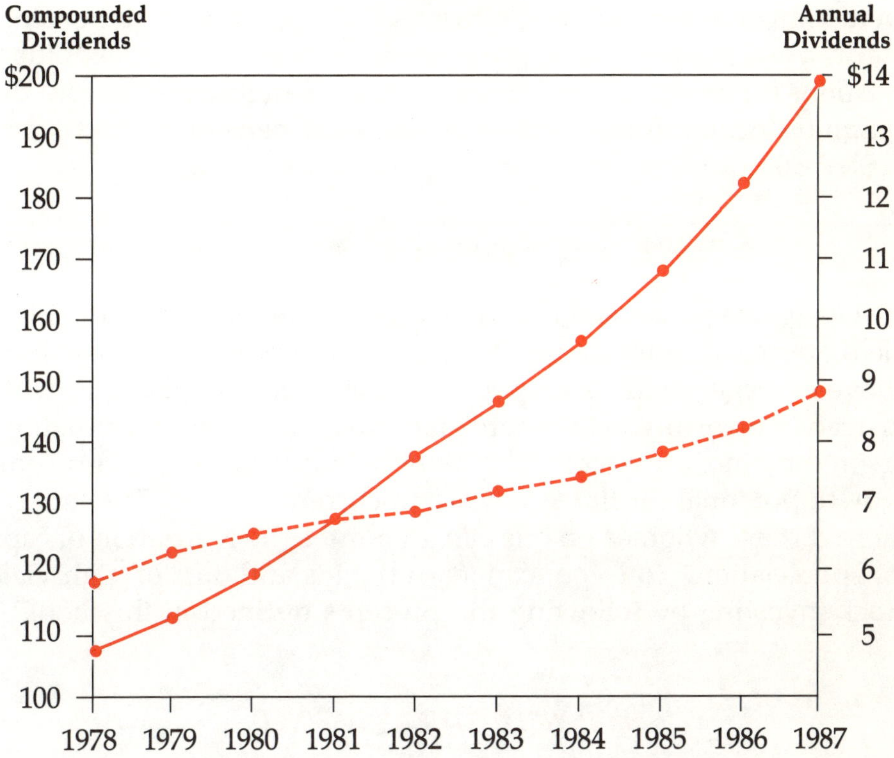

Exhibit 2 shows how the dividends on the Standard and Poors' 500 Composite Index have increased each year and the cumulative effect of compounding those rising dividends, assuming $100 was invested at the beginning of 1978.

Another very important consideration for investors is that the share prices of higher-yielding securities are usually less volatile than other equities. That's because the yield acts as a floor on their price. In the bloodbath of October, 1987, when the Standard & Poor's 500 Stock Index fell 15 percent in just a few days, utility stocks dropped by only 5.4 percent, telephones by 7.6 percent and international oils by 8.2 percent. Each is a high-yielding group of stocks.

Here's one more fact to show the defensive characteristics of high-yield stocks. In the twelve month period beginning before the crash (October 1, 1987 to September 30, 1988), income-oriented mutual funds did quite well compared to the S&P 500. Their total returns were almost 5 percent, while the S&P dropped over 12 percent.

Utility funds	+4.5 percent
Equity-Income funds	+4.8 percent
S&P 500	-12.4 percent

Source: Lipper Analytical Services, Inc.

Many pension fund and mutual fund managers practice the high-yield approach to investing. They concentrate on stocks that have above-average yields and good prospects for dividend growth. Instead of investing in the more glamorous, pure growth situations favored by most investors, the high-yield advocate gives up some growth potential for the assurance of current income. The latter is more certain, whereas no one can guarantee the realization of capital appreciation. You, too, can learn the ins and outs of high-yield stock investing by following the precepts outined in this book.

HIGH-YIELD STOCKS DEFINED

By now you should be asking, ''What are high-yield stocks?'' Generally speaking, they're stocks with cash dividend yields considerably above the average yield for all stocks. The dividend yield is expressed as the current cash dividend divided by the stock's current selling price. Thus, a stock selling for $25 with a $1.50 dividend offers shareholders a 6 percent current yield. If the stock price rises to $27.50, the dividend yield drops to a shade under 5.5 percent; if the price drops to $22.50, the yield rises to 6.7 percent. Note, this is the same inverse relationship of price to yield as with bonds; as the price of the security drops, the yield rises.

The most widely used measurement for the average yield level of common stocks is the Standard and Poor's 500 Composite Stock Index (S&P 500). It is broadly representative of most industries and stocks which trade on the major exchanges. It is a market value-weighted benchmark of common stock performance, which includes 500 companies with the largest market capitalization, measured by shares outstanding multiplied by stock price.

The S&P 500 is subdivided into industrials (400 stocks), utilities (40), transportation (20), and finance (40). Historically, the yield on the S&P 500 has averaged 4.8 percent. The range over the last 30 years has been between 3 percent and 6 percent.

Other yield measures are those of the Dow Jones Industrial Averages (DJIA) and the 1,650 or so stocks covered by the Value Line Investment Survey. All average yields are close and will follow one another, although the DJIA yield will tend to be a bit more generous because the companies in it are a group of larger, more mature, higher-dividend paying companies.

Because the yields of each of the averages move up and down depending on the action of the stock market, it's best to define high-yield stocks in relation to an index yield. An arbitrary definition of high-yield stocks might be those stocks with yields at least 50 percent greater than the average yield for all stocks. In bull markets, when stock prices are rising, the average yields could drop as low as 3 percent. (In 1987, at the height of the bull market before Black Monday, the dividend yield on the S&P 500 fell to an extremely low level of 2.6 percent.) In order to qualify with at least a 50 percent greater return, a high-yield stock would have to yield 4.5 percent. Likewise, if common stock yields rose to 5 percent in a bear market, a high-yield stock would be defined as one providing a current return of 7.5 percent or more.

How can you research what the current yields for the various averages are? You can obtain this information from several periodicals and investment services. The *Wall Street Journal* gives the current yield on the S&P 500, as well as a graph showing the monthly yield for a brief historical period. It appears after the first week every month in the "Investment Insight" section in the lower left corner of the first page of the "Money and Investing" section. The *Standard and Poor's Outlook* lists the S&P yields and the DJIA yields in its "Market Measures" table on the third page of the publication. The *Value Line Investment Survey* shows the yield for its stocks and that of the DJIA in its "Market Monitor" table. The DJIA yield also

Exhibit 3
Common Stock Yields
Monthly yield on the S&P 500, in percent

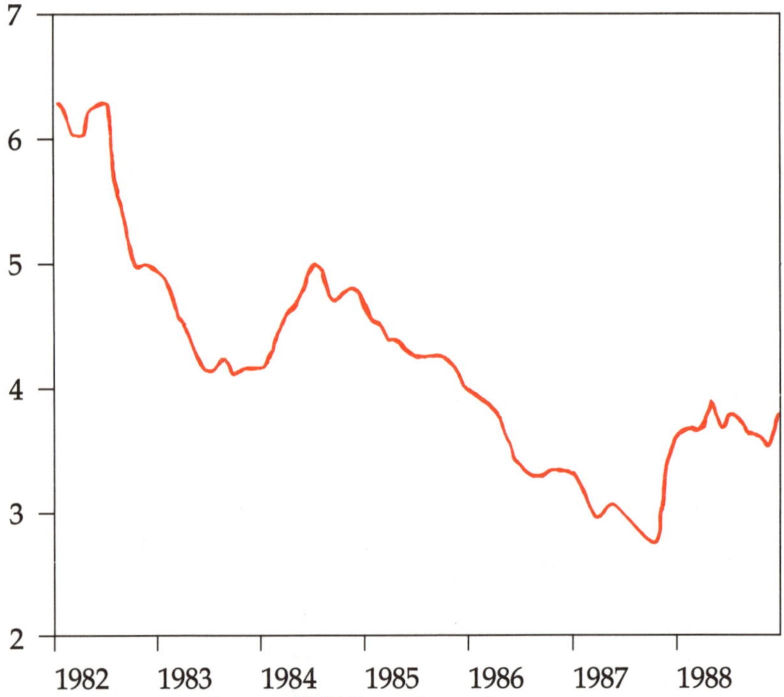

Source: Wall Street Journal

appears weekly in *Barrons* magazine's table "C.I./Yield Gap" located toward the end of the publication.

Exhibit 3 from the *Wall Steet Journal* shows how current yields for the S&P 500 have moved over the past five years.

HIGH-YIELD NOT NECESSARILY HIGH-RISK

Contrary to what many investors believe, investing in stocks with high yields doesn't necessarily translate into assuming unduly high risks. Take, for instance, electric utility companies that pay out a large percentage of earnings to stockholders as cash dividends. Their

Exhibit 4

Year	Yields: S&P 400	Yields: Util. 40	Difference in Yields
1978	5.2	9.2	77%
1979	5.3	9.5	79
1980	4.4	9.7	105
1981	5.4	10.4	93
1982	4.5	9.7	116
1983	3.7	9.5	157
1984	4.1	8.7	112
1985	3.4	7.3	115
1986	3.1	6.3	103
1987	3.1	7.3	135

Source: Standard and Poor's Statistics, 1988

dividends are much higher than those of industrial stocks, as indicated in Exhibit 4 which compares historical yields of the Standard & Poor's 400 industrial stocks with yields of the S&P 40 utility stocks.

Because they're not perceived as pure growth companies, electric utility stocks are reasonably priced compared to the rest of the market. They sport dividend yields 50 percent to 100 percent higher than the market average. Most receive high-quality marks from the rating services and have a history of low price volatility. (Utilities with nuclear plant problems are the exception.)

SEARCHING FOR HIGH-YIELD STOCKS

Plenty of common stocks of solid, conservative companies provide relatively high yields for their shareholders. You can narrow your search considerably because they are concentrated in certain industries. These include natural gas distributors and pipelines, electric utilities, telephone companies, insurance companies, money center and regional commercial banks, real estate investment trusts as well as blue chip companies in a variety of other industries.

Many high-yielding stocks also have good capital gain possibilities, for increasing dividends tend to have a positive impact on stock prices. Specific industry groups with high-yield stocks are discussed in the second half of the book, along with information on how you should go about analyzing the individual companies.

The *Value Line Investment Survey* publishes a list of the highest yielding non-utility stocks based on estimated year-ahead dividends. As you can see, a large number of these stocks are of companies which fall into the above-named industry groups.

It should be noted that for purposes of our discussion, high-yield stocks do not include the more speculative high yields associated with stocks where a dividend cut is imminent, or where the prospect

Exhibit 5
Highest Yielding Non-Utility Stocks
(Based upon estimated year-ahead dividends per share)

		Timeliness		Current			
Page No.	Stock Name	Recent Price	Safety Rank	P/E Ratio	Est'd Yield	Industry Group	Industry Rank
1836	Mesa Ltd. Part.	13	- 4	33.3	15.4%	Petroleum (Producing)	73
1177	Lomas & Nettelton Mtg.	18	4 3	7.1	14.2%	R.E.I.T.	90
1843	Transco Expl. Partners	5 5/8	- 4	NMF	13.4%	Petroleum (Producing)	73
1831	Enserch Expl. Partners	9 3/8	- 3	17.7	12.8%†	Petroleum (Producing)	73
1215	Blyvoor Gold ADR	3 5/8	- 4	8.0	12.5%	Gold/Diamond (S.A.)	—
1218	Free State Consol.	7 5/8	- 4	8.0	12.5%	Gold/Diamond (S.A.)	.
1180	Mortgage & Ritty Trust	17	3 3	8.8	11.8%	R.E.I.T.	90
2138	United Kingdom Fund	9 3/8	- 3	NMF	11.7%	Unassigned	—
1176	L&N Housing	15	5 2	NMF	11.7%	R.E.I.T.	90
2028	Manufacturers Hanover	29	3 3	3.5	11.3%	Bank	39
888	Standard Pacific, L.P.	12	1 4	5.1	11.3%	Homebuilding	37
667	Koger Properties	25	3 3	27.2	11.2%	Real Estate	84
978	Amer. Capital Bond Fund	20	3 2	NMF	11.0%	Investment Co. (Income)	53
885	NVRyan L.P.	6	2 4	4.9	10.8%	Homebuilding	37
2134	Duff & Phelps	7 7/8	- 2	NMF	10.8%	Unassigned	—
979	1838 Bond-Debenture	18	3 1	NMF	10.8%	Investment Co. (Income)	53
2057	Lomas Financial Corp.	13	4 3	11.3	10.8%†	Financial Services	71
2091	ASA Ltd.	38	3 3	NMF	10.5%	Investment Co. (Domestic)	49
1845	Union Expl. Partners	13	- 3	16.9	10.4%	Petroleum (Producing)	73
982	Mut'l of Omaha Int Sh	14	3 1	NMF	10.4%	Investment Co. (Income)	53

Exhibit 5
Highest Yielding Non-Utility Stocks (Cont'd.)
(Based upon estimated year-ahead dividends per share)

Page No.	Stock Name	Recent Price	Timeliness	Safety Rank	Current P/E Ratio	Est'd Yield	Industry Group	Industry Rank
980	Hancock (John) Invs. Tr.	20	3	1	NMF	10.3%	Investment Co. (Income)	53
961	Montgomery St Inc Sec	18	3	1	NMF	10.3%	Investment Co. (Income)	53
415	Occidental Petroleum	26	3	3	16.3	9.6%	Petroleum (Integrated)	56
636	USF&G Corp.	29	3	2	9.5	9.5%	Insurance (Prop/Casualty)	30
1217	Driefontein (ADR)	8 1/2	-	4	10.6	9.4%	Gold/Diamond (S.A.)	—
2135	Global Yield Fund	9 3/8	-	3	NMF	9.0%	Unassigned	—
1178	MGI Properties	18	4	2	10.7	8.9%	R.E.I.T.	90
619	G't Northern Iron	35	3	3	9.8	8.9%	Metals & Mining (Ind'l)	4
2011	Chemical Banking Corp.	31	2	3	3.6	8.8%	Bank	39
1179	MONY Real Estate Inv.	8 1/4	-	2	18.4	8.7%	R.E.I.T.	90
1174	First Union Real Est.	18	5	2	13.1	8.6%	R.E.I.T.	90
1216	De Beers Consol.	11	-	3	4.0	8.6%	Gold/Diamond (S.A.)	—
647	First Bank System	20	5	3	NMF	8.5%	Bank (Midwest)	43
1220	Western Deep Lev.	27	-	4	10.8	8.5%	Gold/Diamond (S.A.)	—
1840	Sun Energy Partners	12	-	4	NMF	8.3%	Petroleum (Producing)	73
1175	HRE Properties	22	3	2	20.2	8.2%	R.E.I.T.	90
1182	Property Capital Trust	21	-	2	9.6	8.1%	R.E.I.T.	90
2040	Sterling Bancorp	10	3	3	12.2	8.0%	Bank	39
2010	Chase Manhattan	29	2	3	2.6	7.9%	Bank	39
623	Cont'l Corp.	33	3	2	11.1	7.9%	Insurance (Prop/Casualty)	30
1219	Kloof Gold Mng ADR	8 1/4	-	4	12.8	7.8%	Gold/Diamond (S.A.)	—
2093	Gaebelli Equity	9 3/4	-	3	NMF	7.7%	Investment Co. (Domestic)	49
457	Panhandle Eastern	26	3	3	26.5	7.7%	Natural Gas (Diversified)	64
359	ServiceMaster L.P.	23	-	3	11.3	7.7%	Industrial Services	44
1172	BRE Properties	31	3	2	14.4	7.7%	R.E.I.T.	90
1166	Imperial Corp. of Amer.	8 3/4	3	5	2.8	7.7%	Thrift	72
983	Nuveen Muni Value Fund	9 5/8	-	2	NMF	7.6%	Investment Co. (Income)	
421	Shell Transport	36	4	1	10.5	7.6%	Petroleum (Integrated)	56
2061	Hallwood Group	15	3	5	7.5	7.5%	Financial Services	71
820	BET PLC (ADR)	16	3	3	10.7	7.5%	European Diversified	28
2097	Liberty All-Star	7 1/4	-	3	NMF	7.5%	Investment Co. (Domestic)	49
2019	First Fidelity Bancorp	27	5	1	51.9	7.5%	Bank	
105	Gen'l Motors	85	2	1	6.1	7.1%	Auto & Truck	46
2089	Travelers Corp.	35	4	2	10.3	7.1%	Insurance (Diversified)	60
682	Reliance Group Holdings	4 5/8	4	4	13.5	7.0%	Unassigned	—
420	Royal Dutch Petr.	57	4	1	9.5	7.0%	Petroleum (Integrated)	56
370	Scandinavia Fund	6 1/2	-	3	NMF	6.9%	Investment Co. (Foreign)	—
459	Sonat Inc.	29	3	3	17.7	6.9%	Natural Gas (Diversified)	64
904	Lone Star Inds.	28	4	3	NMF	6.8%	Cement	89
641	Boatmen's Bancshs.	31	4	1	7.0	6.8%	Bank (Midwest)	

Exhibit 5
Highest Yielding Non-Utility Stocks (Cont'd.)
(Based upon estimated year-ahead dividends per share)

Page No.	Stock Name	Recent Price	Timeliness	Safety Rank	Current P/E Ratio	Est'd Yield	Industry Group	Industry Rank
2101	Regional Fin'l Shs.	6	-	2	NMF	6.7%	Investment Co. (Domestic)	49
1858	McDermott Int'l	15	4	3	NMF	6.7%	Oilfield Services/Equip.	79
2020	First Interstate Bancorp	44	3	3	23.4	6.7%	Bank	39
450	Enron Corp.	37	3	3	NMF	6.7%†	Natural Gas (Diversified)	64
634	Seibels Bruce Group	12	3	3	6.7	6.7%	Insurance (Prop/Casualty)	30
110	PACCAR Inc.	40	2	3	7.7	6.6%	Auto & Truck	46
258	British Airways (ADR)	29	-	3	5.5	6.6%	Air Transport	18
2047	Zions Bancorp.	22	4	3	NMF	6.5%	Bank	39
407	British Petroleum PLC	54	4	2	13.0	6.5%	Petroleum (Integrated)	56
2006	Bank of New England	22	3	3	5.0	6.5%	Bank	39
1162	GLENFED Inc.	20	3	3	3.8	6.5%	Thrift	72
2078	CIGNA Corp.	47	3	2	11.0	6.5%	Insurance (Diversified)	60
1155	CalFed Inc.	22	4	3	3.9	6.4%	Thrift	72
2026	KeyCorp	20	4	2	5.9	6.4%	Bank	39
1173	Federal Ritty. Inv. Trust	21	5	2	77.8	6.4%	R.E.I.T.	90
1181	New Plan R'lty Trust	16	3	2	16.0	6.4%	R.E.I.T.	90
1510	Kroger Co.	8 3/4	-	4	NMF	6.4%	Grocery	17
2045	Valley National	24	3	2	6.3	6.3%	Bank	39
1183	Santa Anita Realty	33	3	3	16.8	6.3%	R.E.I.T.	90
2030	Meridia Bancorp.	19	3	1	7.6	6.2%	Bank	39
831	Phillips NV (NY Shs)	17	3	3	11.6	6.2%	European Diversified	28
460	Tenneco, Inc.	49	3	3	18.8	6.2%	Natural Gas (Diversified)	64
1896	B.A.T. Inds. (ADR)	8	3	3	7.0	6.1%	Unassigned	—
1019	Joslyn Corp.	27	3	2	9.5	6.1%	Electrical Equipment	67
2073	Aetna Life & Casualty	47	3	1	8.3	6.1%	Insurance (Diversified)	60
2059	Green Tree	10	5	3	7.8	6.0%	Financial Services	71
591	Fansteel Inc.	10	3	3	10.2	6.0%	Metal Fabricating	40
365	First Australia Fund	8 3/8	-	3	NMF	6.0%	Investment Co. (Foreign)	—
2012	Citicorp	26	3	3	4.6	6.0%	Bank	39
104	Ford Motor	51	2	3	4.6	5.9%	Auto & Truck	46
1214	Anglo Amer. Cp S.A.	16	-	3	8.2	5.9%	Gold/Diamond (S.A.)	—
1005	Core Inds.	12	3	3	10.3	5.9%	Electrical Equipment	67
2035	Security Pacific	35	3	3	5.1	5.9%	Bank	39
826	Hanson PLC (ADR)	14	1	3	7.0	5.9%	European Diversified	28
424	Texaco Inc.	51	3	3	14.2	5.9%	Petroleum (Integrated)	56

† Dividend cut possible.

is fairly good for a dividend cut or omission sometime down the road. Here the high yields are red flags that denote high risk. In the *Value Line* chart on page 10, focus on the "+" sign appearing next to those companies whose dividends are expected to be cut. These are superficially high yields based on past dividends. If and when the dividend is cut, the yield will fall dramatically.

High-yield stocks should not be equated with high-yield bonds (often referred to as junk bonds) which are very popular among certain investors. Junk bonds with yields of five percentage points or more above Treasury bond yields are usually issued by two types of companies: either large corporations with extremely leveraged balance sheets or small growth companies with no track record. The bond investors hope that cash flows will be adequate to cover the interest payments. Shareholders of these risky companies can expect to receive little or no dividends.

On the other hand, high-yield stock investors are investing in stocks of mature companies in stable industries with good cash flows, a long history of dividend payments, and a stock price that's reasonable in relation to earnings and book value. Clearly these are not speculative securities.

BOND SUBSTITUTES

Professional portfolio managers and other sophisticated investors often view high-yield stocks as bond substitutes with a capital appreciation kicker. The prices of both high-yield stocks and bonds are subject to changes in interest rate levels, but price swings are less pronounced than for stocks in general. The interest income from a bond, represented by the coupon rate, is fixed and can never go higher. A $1,000 bond with an 8 percent coupon will always pay the owner $80 a year until maturity, never more and never less, except if it happens to go into default.

The dividend yield on a high-yield stock is usually lower than on a bond. However, cash dividends paid on the stock may go up each year as company earnings increase. Therefore, the high-yield investor has a chance of seeing the dividend yield, as measured by his purchase price, increase over time. At some point it will exceed

Exhibit 6

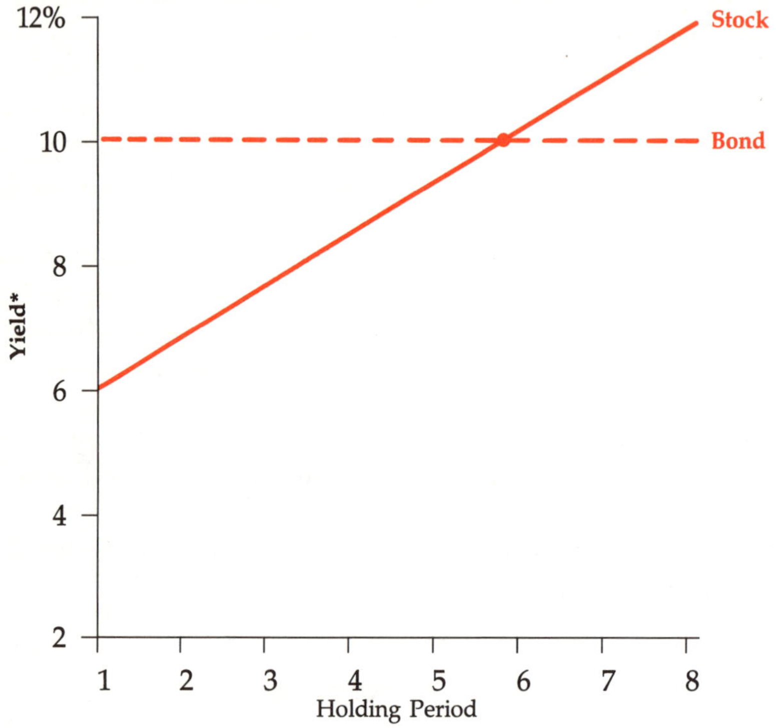

*Based on bond or purchase price.

the yield on the bond (yields based on stock and bond purchase prices), as shown in Exhibit 6. In addition, higher earnings and dividends often translate into higher stock prices down the road, making for even greater returns.

IMPACT OF TAX REFORM

Before passage of the Tax Reform Act of 1986, many individual investors had good reason to choose a growth stock investment strategy over a high-yield stock strategy — favorable tax treatment for capital gain-derived income. Prior to 1987, a 60 percent exclusion of capital gain income was allowed, with the 40 percent balance of the gain taxed at regular rates. Therefore, taxpayers in the 50 percent bracket paid only a 20 percent tax on capital gains arising from security sales (50 percent times 40 percent of the taxable gain).

Meanwhile, ordinary income, such as interest and dividend payments, was taxed 100 percent. The 50 percent bracket investor paid fifty cents in taxes on every dollar of ordinary income. Given this situation, high tax bracket shareholders opted to invest for capital gain income to raise their after-tax returns.

Tax reform dramatically changed this strategy. All income is taxed at 28 percent (33 percent for high earners) regardless of source. Ordinary income will no longer cost more in taxes than capital gain income. The high-yield stock investment strategy has clearly become more attractive with its emphasis on the greater certainty of the receipt of current income versus capital gain income.

Exhibit seven shows the impact of the Tax Reform Act on individual and corporate tax rates:

Exhibit 7
Tax rate Changes after Reform

	Before Reform		After Reform
	Ordinary Income	Capital Gain Income	All Income
Individuals	50%	20%	28%*
Corporations	46	28	34

*33 percent for single and married persons with taxable income between $43,150 and $89,560, and between $71,900 and $149,250 respectively, then dropping to 28 percent again. These brackets will be adjusted upward for inflation beginning in 1989.

The impact of tax reform on investing can be more clearly shown by comparing the after-tax returns from a current income-oriented investment and a growth investment, both of which are expected to generate a 12 percent total return. The return on the former was comprised of 8 percent current income and 4 percent capital appreciation, while all the return on the growth investment was from appreciation. Assume that the investor was in the highest possible tax brackets of 50 percent before tax reform and 33 percent after reform:

Exhibit 8
Comparison of Returns from Income and Growth Investments

	Before-Tax Returns		After-Tax Returns	
	Current Return	Capital Apprec.	Before Reform	After Reform
Income Investment	8.0%	4.0%	7.0%	8.0%
Growth Investment	—	12.0	9.6	8.0

As can be seen by Exhibit 8, the ''before tax reform'' advantage was clearly with the growth investment, which had a 9.6 percent return compared with a 7 percent return for the income investment. The after-tax return on the income investment increases from 7.0 percent to 8.0 percent under tax reform, while the return for the growth investment declines from 9.6 percent to 8.0 percent. Both returns are now equal. The only difference is that you can defer taxes on capital appreciation as long as you don't sell the security, whereas with current income, you pay taxes on it when received. But this advantage is slight, except in the case of long-term holds of five to ten years or more.

The Tax Reform Act of 1986 will eventually bring another plus to high-yield stock investors. Before tax reform, many corporations retained a large portion of earnings to plow back into the business. If they could earn more on these additional company assets than shareholders could on any after-tax dividend income, then rising corporate earnings could, in effect, be transformed into capital gain. This assumes the capitalization rate (price-earnings ratio, or the price investors are willing to pay for each dollar of earnings) stayed the same. As indicated earlier, with the 60 percent exclusion, capital gain income was markedly better than dividend income for most investors. It was taxed at a maximum rate of 20 percent rather than 50 percent.

Tax reform has given several incentives for public companies to raise dividends, thus making their shares more attractive to high-yield stock investors. Corporate tax rates have dropped from 46 percent to 34 percent (see chart on page 20), giving companies greater after-tax cash flow. Individual tax rates are lower, which means current dividend income is more valuable to shareholders on an after-tax basis. Finally, the previously mentioned loss of the capital gains deduction makes reaching for capital gains a less attractive proposition for investors. Clearly, there's less incentive to take on more risk if the tax rates are the same for both types of investment income.

BENEFITS OF HIGH-YIELD STOCK INVESTING

What are the benefits from high-yield stock investing? First, these stocks provide you with downside protection for your portfolio during a general drop in security prices because their yield acts to support the price. In a market slide of 25 percent, stocks with above-average dividend yields, and good prospects for dividend increases, should drop only 10 percent to 15 percent. High-yield stock investing is a defensive strategy almost synonymous with capital preservation.

Next comes lower risk than through investing in either pure growth or pure current income situations. Growth stock investors are much more subject to the ups and downs of the economy, the stock market and corporate earnings surprises. Fixed-income investors are at the mercy of interest rate movements.

High-yield stock investors, on the other hand, are blessed with the best of both worlds. They receive high current income to offset losses from stock market drops. Although the prices of high-yield stocks are clearly susceptible to changes in the general level of interest rates, the possibility of dividend growth over time partially mitigates this concern. If the dividend increases, the price does not have to drop very much to keep pace with yields on alternative investments in a rising interest rate environment. (A 10 percent increase in the dividend of a high-yielding stock is the equivalent of a 1/2 to 3/4 percent increase in interest rates.)

The fact that a company can consistently raise its dividend helps provide a cushion for the stock during weak markets. The dividend creates a floor against further price deterioration. If the dividend increases in a falling market, the chances are good that more investors will eventually be attracted to the stock because of its sound fundamentals. There's no better defense in a declining stock market than a growing stream of income.

A third benefit of high-yield stock investing is that with less risk comes lower portfolio volatility. The stock prices of dividend paying companies are fairly stable, whereas those of growth companies have more pronounced percentage movements both up and down. Therefore, the aggregate value of a high-yield stock portfolio shouldn't fluctuate as much as other portfolios.

Using investment jargon, high-yield stocks tend to have low betas. "Beta" is the term used by security analysts to portray a quantitative expression of the volatility of a stock's price in relation to the stock market as a whole. A beta of 1.5 indicates a rise and fall of 15 percent for every 10 percent change in the stock market; a beta of 0.8 indicates an 8 percent movement up and down for every 10 percent change. More conservative high-yield stocks have betas in the 0.75 to 0.90 range, while growth stocks carry betas of 1.05 to as high as 1.30.

A fourth benefit from investing in high-yield stocks is that they are usually reasonably valued vis-a-vis the rest of the stock market, thus providing another damper on volatility. With lower price-earnings ratios and low price-to-book value ratios, high-yield stocks are less expensive in terms of what investors pay for each dollar of earnings and assets. As a result, negative earnings surprises or other bad corporate news have less impact on the prices of high-yield stocks.

A fifth benefit from high-yield stock investing is that its proponents tend to hold their stocks for the long-term to realize increasing yields and higher total returns. They do less trading than other investors, which reduces high transaction costs associated with frequent buying and selling of securities. A buy and hold investment strategy also defers income taxes on capital gain because taxes are not paid until the gains are realized through stock sales.

Naturally, some events may cause higher trading activity such as early achievement of appreciation objectives, or a rapid deterioration in a company's finances. But these will be the exception, rather than the rule. As the old Wall Street saying goes, "slow and steady usually wins the investment race."

A final benefit to the high-yield stock investor is the certainty of cash dividends, which are much more likely to be received than share price appreciation. Simply put, a dollar of income today is worth more than a dollar of capital gain tomorrow. The latter has much greater risk associated with its eventual realization, whereas the former is assured, assuming no surprise cuts by the board of directors. Moreover, while the price of stock rises and falls in response to short-term earnings and market fluctuations, changes in dividends are less volatile. And the vast majority of dividend decisions of corporate management relate to increasing, not reducing, the dividend.

It appears that investors are willing to pay more in the market place for the certainty of current income over the uncertainty of capital appreciation. Witness the price action of publicly-traded "dual" funds—closed-end investment companies that own a portfolio of common stocks. The dual funds have two classes of owners: income shareholders who are entitled to all the income from the portfolio, and growth shareholders who receive all capital appreciation when the fund is liquidated.

Interestingly, the income shares of dual funds sell at premiums to net asset values (NAV), while the growth shares sell at discounts to NAVs. This phenomenon is true for all dual funds. The public clearly values current income more highly than potential capital gains. Fortunately, high-yield stock investors can get these same benefits as dual fund income shareholders without paying any premiums.

In the next chapter we will review the risks of, and rewards from, investing in high-yield stocks.

Chapter Two

RISKS AND RETURNS FROM HIGH-YIELD STOCKS

A thorough knowledge and understanding of the relationship of risk to reward is basic to any investment strategy you use, and high-yield stock investing is no exception. As a rule, when the potential for reward from an investment rises, the risks associated with it also rise. When risks drop, expected returns also drop. This direct relationship is clearly illustrated in Exhibit 1 on page 24.

Simply put, there's no such thing as the proverbial ''free lunch'' for investors — a low-risk, high-return investment. If the perfect one did exist, then investors would rush in and bid its price up. Expected returns would drop to levels more in keeping with a lower-risk investment.

The goal of nearly all investors is to maximize returns for a given level of risk. As a high-yield investor, you should be willing to accept slightly lower long-term returns in exchange for greatly reduced risk. In effect, you are shifting the risk-return line downward. As shown by Exhibit 2 on page 24, the high-yield investor has lower risk for the same returns all along the line.

Exhibit 1
Risk-Reward Relationship

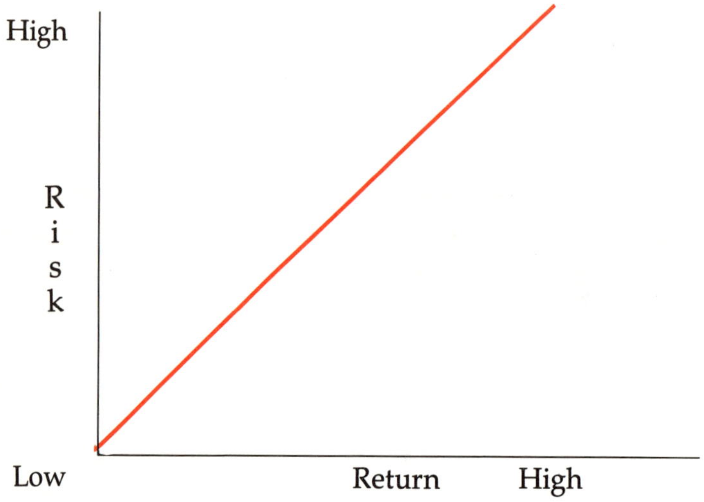

Exhibit 2
Shifting Risk Downward

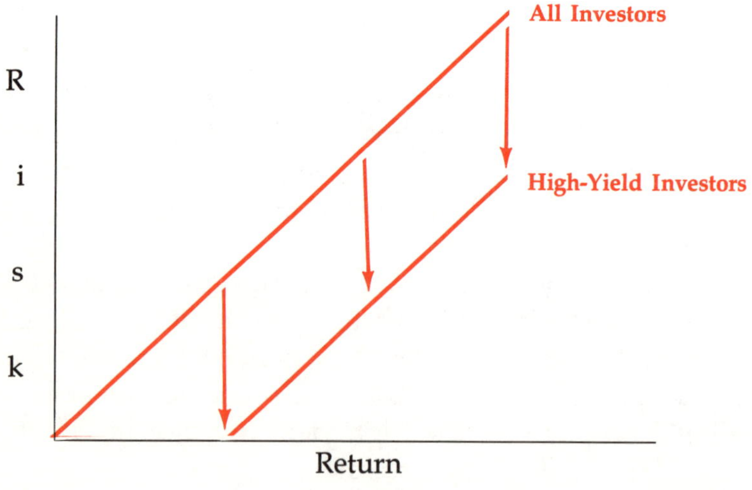

RETURNS FROM STOCKS

As mentioned in the previous chapter, investments produce what are known as "total returns". Part of the total return comes in the form of current income and part is from capital appreciation (or depreciation, in the case of a poor investment). For stocks, the current income component is received in the form of dividends, while the appreciation component is either realized or unrealized, depending on whether the security has been sold or is still held.

HIGH-YIELD STOCK RETURNS—The typical high-yield stock produces higher current income, but offers lower capital gain potential than the stocks of pure growth companies. A good portion of corporate earnings are returned to investors in the form of dividends, rather than plowed back into company assets to enhance future earnings growth.

Expected total returns from a typical high-yield stock are shown by the simplified table in Exhibit 3. It's assumed that the dividend increases 3 percent per year to provide the stable 7 percent yield and the stock price increases in line with the dividend growth rate. (In calculating total returns, each year's current yield is based on that year's dividend divided by the beginning year's price.) Annual total returns for the high-yield stock are 10 percent.

With a large portion of the total return component coming from dividends, the total returns are relatively easy to project.

Exhibit 3
Expected Total Returns from a High-Yield Stock

Year	Current Income	Capital Appreciation	Total Return
1	7%	3%	10%
2	7	3	10
3	7	3	10
4	7	3	10
5	7	3	10

GROWTH STOCK RETURNS—Unlike companies with high-yielding stocks, growth companies plow a majority of earnings back into their operations to produce higher future profits, rather than paying out a large portion to shareholders as dividends. Investors bid up their share prices now in anticipation of the receipt of higher dividends later. Higher share prices with low dividend payouts translate into lower current yields.

Exhibit 4 shows the expected returns from a hypothetical growth security over a five-year period. The projections for the growth stock are 2 percent in current yield and 10 percent in annual capital appreciation. It's assumed that the dividend also goes up 10 percent each year to provide the stable 2 percent yield. Total annual returns add up to 12 percent.

Exhibit 4
Expected Total Returns from a Growth Stock

Year	Current Income	Capital Appreciation	Total Return
1	2%	10%	12%
2	2	10	12
3	2	10	12
4	2	10	12
5	2	10	12

Note that these total return figures for the growth stock are slightly more than for the high-yield stock. The risks are also greater, for there's no guarantee that the capital appreciation component will ever be achieved. Stock market conditions control this, as well as the company's future earnings performance. It is also difficult to make return projections for a growth stock. Although the capital appreciation component shown above is steady for purposes of illustration, in reality, the returns will more likely fluctuate from year to year. This outcome was shown in the historical total return graph in Exhibit 1 of the previous chapter.

In summary, expect lower, but steadier, total returns from a high-yield stock compared to a growth stock. That's because a higher portion of the returns is received up front in the form of dividends, and less reliance is placed on uncertain appreciation components of the total return equation.

INVESTMENT RISKS OF HIGH-YIELD STOCKS

Despite their defensive characteristics, you shouldn't be led into a false sense of security that high-yield stocks are free of any investment risks. High-yield stocks do carry certain risks. The objective is to control these risks through proper security selection and portfolio diversification.

For high-yield stock investors, the most worrisome risks are business risk and interest rate risk. Market risk and industry risk are secondary concerns, especially when high-yield stocks are held for the long term and investors aren't forced to sell at inopportune times.

BUSINESS RISK—Business risk relates to the chance that a company experiences an earnings downturn, or deteriorating cash flow, which adversely affects the dividend. Such financial weakness usually causes security values to decline. If the investor fails to anticipate these adverse events, he will suffer a capital loss.

Business risk is present with every security no matter what investment strategy is employed. It can affect the prices of a company's bonds, as well as its stocks. In the worst case scenario of a business bankruptcy, nearly all of the investors' money may be lost.

The chart below shows how the dividend yield is affected when a company with a high-yield stock experiences financial difficulties. The price of the stock reacts first, dropping as the negative news is released to the financial community. The dividend isn't cut right away because the company's board of directors is reluctant to take any drastic action unless the financial condition is extremely precarious.

As the price drops, the yield increases because it's based on the most recent, not future, dividend payments. Finally, when the situation deteriorates, and the directors decide to cut the dividend,

Exhibit 5
Effect of Dividend Cut on Yield

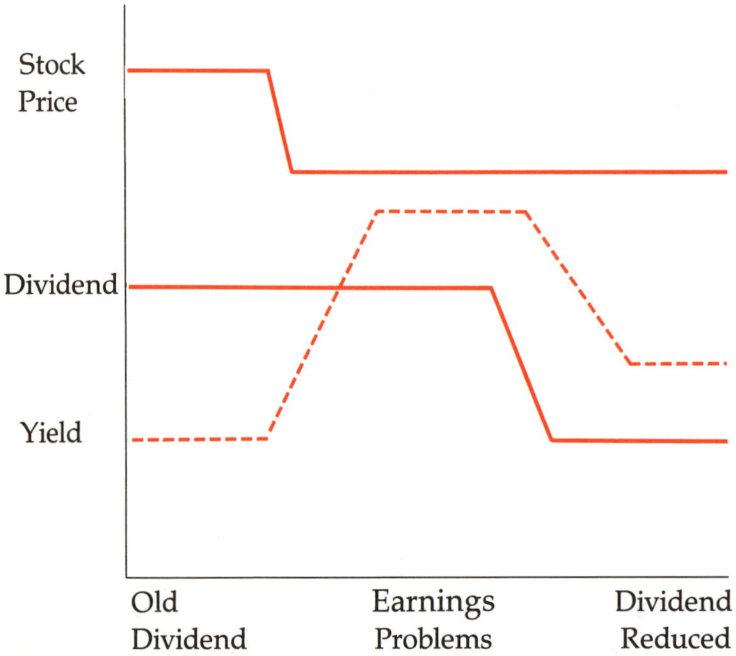

the yield comes back down to somewhere in the neighborhood of where it was before the bad news was released.

In the business risk scenario in Exhibit 5, the high-yield stock investor suffers in two ways: the dividend is reduced, and the stock price drops. However, growth stock investors are exposed to more business risk, and suffer greater losses, as stock prices of these companies will drop even further in reaction to negative business developments. Because they're expensive on a price-earnings basis, they have further to fall when growth is interrupted.

High-yield stock investors can reduce business risk through proper portfolio diversification. This means holding a variety of stocks, at least 10, but preferably 15 or 20. If one company runs into trouble, the impact on the total portfolio is small.

INTEREST RATE RISK—Interest rate risk is a very real concern for high-yield stock investors, as it is for all equity investors. Stock prices respond to broad movements in interest rates because of the impact the cost of money has on the economic outlook. The correlation has been even closer in recent years where pronounced movements of interest rates have greatly affected the business cycle and the stock market.

As a rule, when interest rates rise, stock prices drop. Investors perceive that higher interest rates may choke the economy and adversely impact corporate earnings. As interest rates move up, fixed-income securities become a more attractive investment alternative to stocks. Therefore, investors move money from the stock market to the bond market in search of higher yields; this has a depressing effect on stock prices. When interest rates move down, the reverse happens.

Exhibit 6
Movement of Interest Rates and High-Yield Stocks

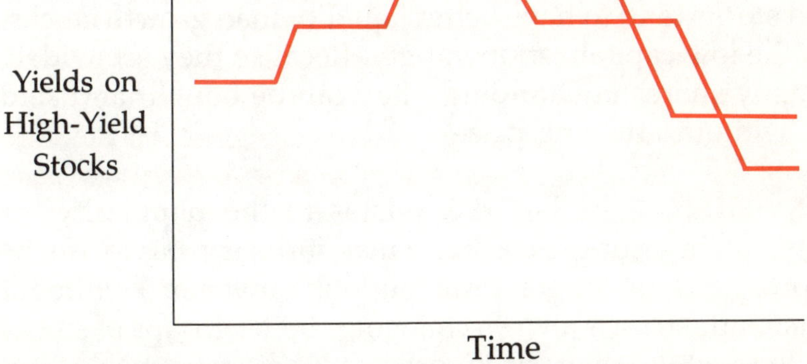

The stocks of companies in the electric utility, telephone and real estate industries are most sensitive to changes in interest rates. Their yields have an 80 percent to 90 percent correlation to movements in the yields of AA utility bonds and 10-year government bonds. That's why they're often characterized by Wall Street as bond substitutes. Witness what happened during April, 1987, when interest rates quickly bounced upward in an attempt by the Federal Reserve to defend the weak U.S. dollar in international markets. The Dow-Jones utility share averages declined by 15 percent in a very short period of time, while the rest of the stock market dipped only slightly.

The relationship between the movement of interest rates and yields on high-yield stocks is shown in Exhibit 6. Changes in stock yields often lag those for bond yields by several weeks.

Although the prices of high-yield stocks are susceptible to similar interest rate risks as bonds, it's not quite to the same degree over the longer term. That's because a growing stream of dividends helps offset a higher interest rate environment by providing higher current yields to the shareholder.

MARKET RISK—Market risk relates to fluctuations in the stock market, as measured by the popular averages, namely the Dow-Jones Industrial Average, the S&P 500 Index, or the New York Stock Exchange Index. For high-yield stock investors, as with all equity investors, this is an important risk to consider. The price of nearly every security is sensitive to stock market movements. With high-yield stock securities, however, market risk is reduced because higher yields provide a cushion against downward price movements.

High-yield stocks tend to have better liquidity than growth stocks, particularly the low capitalization variety. Because they are widely held with many shares outstanding, they can be bought and sold quite easily without affecting price.

INDUSTRY RISK—One last risk relates to the popularity, or unpopularity, of investing in a particular industry based on its near-term prospects or longer term outlook. Investor sentiment toward certain industries is always changing. Some groups of stocks are in favor for a while, then are ignored as others take their place.

This rotation of sector popularity is a basic stock market phenomenon.

High-yield stock industries are susceptible to changing investor sentiment. Electric utilities are out-of-favor when nuclear problems arise, yet they're in favor when the general economic outlook is gloomy. Insurance company stocks go into the dog house when underwriting ratios deteriorate. Telephone company stocks become popular when investors recognize the exceptional earnings potential for their cable TV and cellular radio operations.

High-yield investors have a bit of a problem eliminating industry risk because because many high-yield stocks are concentrated in only a few industries. You don't want to invest at the peak of an industry's popularity. Although it's difficult, you should try to make your investment commitment to an industry near the bottom of the cycle. You also must diversify into as many industries as possible. This can be done by selecting high-yield stocks outside the traditional high-yield industries.

Exhibit 7
Relative Risks and Returns for Growth Stocks, High-Yield Stocks, and Bonds

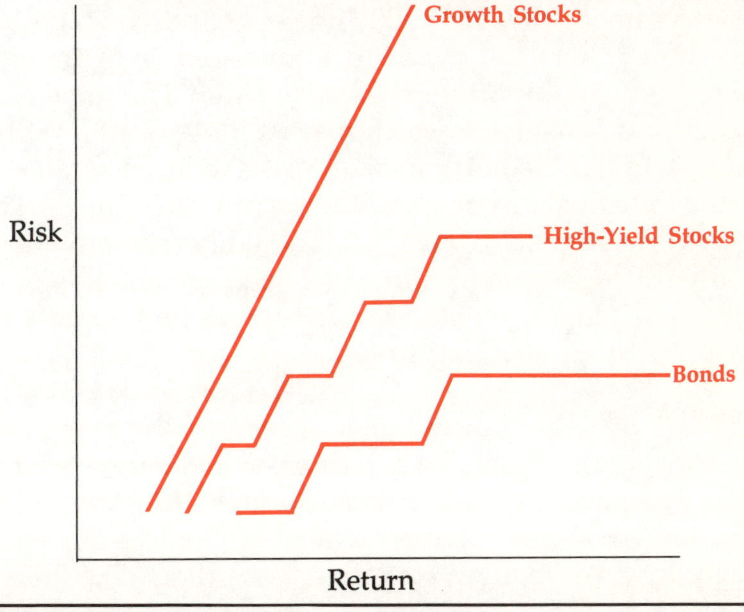

SUMMARY

When it comes to risk and reward characteristics, high-yield stocks fall somewheres in between bonds and growth stocks. Bonds have lower risk and lower returns than high-yield stocks, while growth stocks have higher risk and higher returns. If the risks and returns for each type of security were plotted on a graph, they might look like Exhibit 7 on page 31.

High-yield stock investors take a middle-of-the-road approach to investing. They seek stocks which provide reasonable safety through the generous current yield and a modicum of growth potential from an increasing stream of dividends and dividend reinvestment. This defensive investment strategy is designed to put the risk-reward equation in the investor's favor.

In the next chapter, we'll delve deeper into the whys and wherefores of the common stock dividend — how it helps determine stock prices, how corporate dividend policy is set, and why dividend growth is important to investment success with high-yielding securities.

Chapter Three

COMMON STOCK DIVIDENDS

As a high-yield stock investor, you should be familiar with how future dividends impact stock prices, and what factors are considered when corporate management sets dividend policy.

STOCK VALUATION

What really determines the price at which a stock sells for in the financial markets? Most experts believe that in the final analysis, it's the expectation of future cash dividends that governs a stock's price. Underlying this theory is the premise that the ability to pay dividends is dependent on a company's capacity to generate earnings.

Stock valuation theory is based on the hypothesis that the price of a share of common stock equals the present value of its future stream of dividends. Future dividends are discounted to their present value, with their sum representing the share price an investor should be willing to pay for them.

Here's how the present value concept works. If interest rates remained constant at 10 percent, the present value of a dollar in dividends to be received five years from now is $.62. Reversing the process, if you took today's $.62 and invested it at 10 percent, it will be worth exactly one dollar in five years. The rationale is that a dollar today is worth more than a dollar tomorrow — it is certain, you can earn interest on it, and it will grow in value, whereas a dollar tomorrow will be worth just that — a dollar.

Present value theory can be utilized in stock pricing theory by taking a stream of future dividends and discounting each year's dividend to the present using an appropriate market interest rate. The discount rate might be the current rate for a riskless, short-term Treasury bill or a one-year U.S. government note. Add to this an equity-risk premium for the ownership of common stock. The riskier the stock, the higher the premium. The premium might range from 2 percent for a high-yield stock to 5 percent for a growth stock to 8 percent for a small company high-tech stock.

How do you predict what the future stream of dividends will be? The simplist, and often best, yardstick is past history. Take a company's recent earnings and dividend data, and extrapolate it into the future using an appropriate growth rate. Examine the company's prior record for yearly variations in earnings and dividends and factor this into your projections, along with any other knowledge you might have about the company's prospects.

Theoretically, each company's stock ought to sell for the sum of the present value of all future dividends. If it's higher, then the stock is overpriced and should be avoided. If the stock sells below the sum of the discounted future dividends, then it should be considered for purchase. This arithmetic is illustrated by the following equations, where it's assumed that the common stock cash dividend increases at 6 percent per year.

FUTURE YEAR DIVIDENDS

End of Year:	1	2	3	4	5	6	....
V =	$1.06 +	$1.12 +	$1.19 +	$1.26 +	$1.34 +	$1.42 +	....

"V" is the current value of the stock and the numbers to the right of the equal sign represent the future stream of annual dividends that the common stock will generate for the investor. This future stream must be discounted to its present value by using an appropriate interest rate. A 10 percent rate is shown in the equation below. By calculating the present value (PV), the stock is worth $25.00. This is the theoretical value based on the discounted stream of future dividends.

FUTURE YEAR DISCOUNTED DIVIDENDS

Year 1 2 3 4 5 6

PV = $0.96 + $0.93 + $0.89 + $0.86 + $0.83 + $0.80 + ... $19.70
(the sum of all dividends in years thereafter)

PV = $25.00

If the stock sells at $20 per share, then an opportunity for capital appreciation is present. If the stock is priced at $30 per share, this indicates an overvalued situation you'd want to avoid. Naturally, it's difficult to predict a future stream of dividends. The further out in time you go, the less certain the dividend stream is, and the more imprecise the predictions become. Although this is often the case with high-yield stocks, it's more so for stocks of growth companies.

The numbers in the above equations were taken from the compound value and present value financial tables found in many investment textbooks and mathematics books. An easier way for arriving at the same answer is to subtract the expected dividend growth rate from the discount rate. Then convert the difference into decimal form and divide it into the current dividend. The result is the theoretical price of the stock.

In the example above, you would simply take the difference between the 10 percent discount rate and the 6 percent dividend growth rate, which is 4 percent, and divide .04 into the $1.00 dividend. The result is $25, the same per-share price that was computed using the discount tables.

The present value of future dividends, or the discounted dividend approach to valuing stocks, works best with the stocks of companies whose earnings and dividends are fairly predictable. Fortunately, most high-yielding stocks fall into this category. To fine tune the projections, you should also be aware of the company's dividend policy and trends in payouts.

DIVIDEND PAYOUT POLICIES

A company's dividend policy is the board of director's view (based on management's recommendation) as to what portion of company earnings should be paid out to shareholders as dividends. The ratio of dividends to earnings is known as the payout ratio. If a company earns $1.00 per share on its common stock and pays a $.50 dividend for each share, the payout ratio is 50 percent. With a $.25 dividend, the payout ratio drops to 25 percent.

The management of many companies will publicly announce their dividend policy. They try to keep it consistent from year to year, but with major swings in earnings, this will not be posssible unless the dividend is cut when earnings drop. Managements are very reluctant to do this except in an extreme emergency that jeopardizes the financial health of the company. Exhibit 1 shows the effect of fluctuating earnings on the payout ratio.

As can be seen, earnings plunged in the second year to $1.50 per share. Because of the poor performance, the board of directors decided not to raise the dividend. They didn't cut it either, on the

Exhibit 1

Year	EPS*	Dividends	Payout Ratio
1	$2.50	$1.00	40%
2	1.50	1.00	67
3	2.25	1.10	49
4	2.75	1.15	42

*Earnings per share

belief that this slump was only a temporary condition. However, during those two years the dividend payout ratio jumped from 40 percent to 67 percent. It then stabilized near the 40 percent level as earnings improved in subsequent years.

If management isn't on record as to its payout policy, then you can provide your own estimate using the company's historical financial data. It is important to use earnings data that excludes nonrecurring items, for these are not factored into payout considerations. Exclude special dividends as well. They are sometimes made in special cases when earnings are especially good, or, when a nonrecurring earnings windfall is realized by the company. In the above example, the targeted payout ratio is probably in the 40 percent range.

Normally, the ratio doesn't change in the short run, but may change over a period of years. For instance, when a former growth company matures, its payout ratio increases because dividends are increasing at a faster rate than earnings. Or, likewise, when a company sees profitable growth ahead, it may want to conserve cash for large capital expenditures.

As you examine a company's past financial statements, compare the dividend growth rate to the earnings growth rate. Notice what is happening to the payout ratio. If the payout ratio is relatively constant, then the dividend growth rate will match the earnings growth rate. When it is increasing, dividend growth will be higher than earnings growth; when the payout ratio is decreasing, the dividend growth rate is slower. These relationships are expressed in Exhibit 2.

Exhibit 2

Growth Rates		Payout
Div.	EPS	Ratio
5%	5%	Same
7%	5%	Increases
3%	5%	Decreases

Usually there's a lag between increases in company earnings and increases in dividends. Management wants to be certain that the higher level of earnings can be maintained to support a higher dividend before it makes a commitment to elevate the payout to shareholders. The last thing a board of directors wants is to have to reduce dividends during an earnings decline.

Theoretically, management seeks to maximize the wealth of stockholders. In this context, the dividend decision should be made in the best interests of the stockholder. Because management doesn't know who each stockholder is, they set an overall dividend policy. If current shareholders don't agree with it, they'll sell their shares; if other investors like it, they'll buy the shares. If the dividend policy is changed, it may impact the price of the stock, and management will quickly learn whether or not it made the right decision.

Some managements try to compromise between allowing shareholders to receive more immediate returns on their investments and building long-term value for the benefit of shareholders. The former translates into more generous dividends; the latter results in higher corporate retained earnings and future growth. However, management must be sure it can earn high rates of return on the retained earnings.

Dividend policy is also influenced by what other companies are doing in the industry. There's a tendency not to stray too far from the industry norm. Corporate management that sets dividend policy has to take into consideration the availability of cash, as well as corporate needs for capital spending and working capital.

Because the Tax Reform Act of 1986 did away with the distinction between current income and capital gain income, tax considerations for individual shareholders should no longer be a significant factor when management decides whether or not to distribute earnings. Before tax reform, corporate management felt that investors were more interested in capital gains because of the favorable tax treatment. Companies would retain earnings to build future earnings which would translate into higher share prices. When shares were sold at a profit, the gains would be taxed at a maximum rate of only 20 percent, as opposed to the 50 percent maximum rate on dividend income.

Earnings paid out as dividends are still subject to double taxation—once by the company and again by the shareholder recipient. Earnings retained are only taxed once. But if they result in higher share prices, taxes on any capital appreciation must be paid when the shares are eventually sold. These tax rates are the same as on ordinary income such as dividends. Therefore, the only tax difference is that with dividends, the tax is paid immediately, whereas with capital gains, the tax can be deferred until the shares are sold. This tax deferral can be a significant benefit, however, if the shares keep increasing in value.

Several legal factors also determine how much earnings a corporation can pay out in cash dividends. The provisions of indenture agreements of corporate bonds limit the amount of the retained earnings account on the balance sheet that can be used for payment of dividends to shareholders. Bank loans may also have similar restrictions. Suppose a company has a retained earnings account of $20 million. A lender may say that if the account falls below $15 million, no dividends may be paid. In order for this to occur, the company would have to sustain losses of over $5 million, for losses reduce the retained earnings account. In this instance, management will have probably already eliminated the dividend to conserve cash.

The choice of how much to pay out in dividends is also governed by a corporation's need to raise external funds through the issuance of debt securities, preferred stock and common stock. Interest must be paid on debt, and dividends must be paid on preferred stock, while the sale of new common stock dilutes existing shareholders' ownership of the corporation. Retained earnings are viewed by many as a "cheap" substitute for external funds; the more that is retained, the less is the reliance placed on outside sources of capital and the lower is the out-of-pocket cost of financing growth.

Finally, the dividend payout ratio also impacts on the creditworthiness of the corporation. By retaining more earnings, the company can reduce its financial leverage. Retained earnings are a part of shareholder equity. When the latter increases and debt remains the same, the debt-equity ratio drops, as shown in the following example where retained earnings increase by $10 million:

	Before	After
Debt	$10,000,000	$10,000,000
Equity	30,000,000	40,000,000
Debt-equity ratio	.33	.25

Lower debt-equity ratios keep the cost of capital down. The optimum ratio is what the commercial bankers and investment bankers believe is proper for the industry, given its sensitivity to the business cycle and other factors.

HIGH VERSUS LOW PAYOUT

A company with a high-yielding stock usually pays out a large percentage of earnings to stockholders in the form of dividends. It usually operates in a stable industry characterized by steady earnings and cash flow. Such a company has little need to retain a large portion of its earnings to finance future growth.

A growth-oriented company, on the other hand, usually pays out a low percentage of earnings in dividends. The bulk of earnings is kept in the business. Retained earnings are used for investment in additional plants and equipment, inventories, or other components of working capital to fuel further growth. If the company has a high return on equity, then earnings that are plowed back into the business bring down more profit to the bottom line.

The hypothetical example below shows how different dividend payout policies affect share price and total returns. A company with $5 million in stockholders' equity, that earns $1 million in net profits, has a 20 percent return on equity. Assume it can generate the same rate of return on additional capital invested in the company. One million shares are outstanding and the stock sells at a price-earnings ratio of 10. The board of directors can pay out either 100 percent of earnings, 50 percent, or nothing. The effects of each payout option on future earnings and shareholder returns are shown in Exhibit 3 on page 43.

The far-right column, with the zero payout to shareholders, shows the highest returns of 20 percent. Conversely, the column with the highest payout shows the lowest total return of 10 percent. On the surface, it looks like the growth/low payout approach is the winner.

But as alluded to previously, shareholders of growth stock companies incur several risks. The first is that the company cannot maintain the high rate of return on its retained earnings. The second risk is that the price-earnings ratio may drop due to stock market

Exhibit 3

	Payout Ratio		
	100%	50%	0%
Stockholders' equity	$5,000,000	$5,000,000	$5,000,000
Addition to retained earnings	0	500,000	1,000,000
New total equity	$5,000,000	$5,500,000	$6,000,000
Next year's earnings*	$1,000,000	$1,100,000	1,200,000
Next year's EPS	$1.00	$1.10	$1.20
Next year's stock price**	$10.00	$11.00	$12.00
Paid to shareholders***	$1.00	$.50	0
Capital appreciation	0	$1.00	$2.00
Total return	$1.00	$1.50	$2.00
Per cent toal return	10%	15%	20%

*Assume 20 percent return on equity.
**Assumes price-earnings ratio stays the same.
***During previous year.

conditions or some other factor. If either event occurs, the stock price won't increase as forecasted in the above illustration.

DIVIDEND SECURITY

A prime concern for high-yield investors is the security of the common stock dividend, particularly during difficult economic times. Although most managements strive to maintain the dividend, there are instances when they will find it absolutely necessary to cut or omit it.

When the dividend payout ratio of 40 percent to 50 percent suddenly rises to 80 percent to 90 percent, you should realize it's a good bet the dividend is vulnerable. In this case, earnings have dropped considerably and management has deferred a negative dividend decision until the last minute. Remember, dividends paid in the past are history; they are not guaranteed in the future until the board of directors declares them.

Dividend cuts usually occur with small capitalization companies. Managements of larger companies will do almost anything to maintain their dividends — slashing the dividend would be viewed as a last resort to save the company. This is because of the prestige factor of having a long history of uninterrupted dividend payments. Also, larger companies can better afford to dip into cash reserves to maintain dividends during periods of temporary business reversals.

DIVIDEND REINVESTMENT PLANS

Many companies have dividend reinvestment plans (DRIPs) to encourage shareholders to keep their dividends invested in the company. This is an excellent opportunity for high-yield investors to plow dividends back into additional shares of stock and take advantage of dollar cost averaging. More shares means more dividends, which mean more shares can be purchased as the magic of compounding dividends comes into play.

With a dividend reinvestment plan, cash dividends are used to either purchase new shares from the company's treasury or existing shares in the secondary market. Stocks with high yields have the most to offer under these programs because large dividends mean more shares can be bought each quarter. And those companies with steadily rising dividends are an even better deal for DRIP participants.

Simply put, DRIPs allow individual shareholders to have their cash dividends automatically reinvested in additional shares of company stock. These purchases are often made without brokerage commissions and sometimes at a discount to market value. When commissions are charged, they are very low because shares are purchased in large blocks at steep discounts. The only drawback is that shares must be held in the shareholder's name, not street (brokerage house) name.

Nearly 1,000 companies offer DRIPs, including three-fourths of all companies included in the S&P 500 Stock Index. Most blue chip, electric utility, natural gas, and telephone companies offer such plans. Appendix D gives more detailed information on the mechanics of how dividend reinvestment plans work.

DIVIDEND GROWTH RATES

When analyzing a high-yield stock, you should pay considerable attention to the growth rate of its dividend. Take the time to calculate the pace at which the dividend has been increasing. Attempt to predict what its future growth rate might be, based on the earnings growth and the payout ratio. Remember, a rising stream of dividends helps insulate a high-yield stock from market drops.

Look at the dividend growth rate over a period of time long enough to include a business cycle from peak to trough back to peak. This will show what happens to the dividend through good times and bad. Measure the growth rate for shorter periods of time to determine whether the percentage increase is accelerating or decelerating.

You should make sure you're calculating compound annual growth rates, not the average annual growth rate. The latter will be higher, but it's not a true reflection of how fast future dividends may grow. This important difference is shown in the example for Company XYZ below, where the $1.00 dividend at the end of year 1 grows to $1.40 in year 5:

Company XYZ

Year	1	2	3	4	5
Dividends	$1.00	1.10	1.18	1.28	1.40

Compound annual growth rate	8.75%
Average annual growth rate	10.0%

The average annual growth rate is calculated by taking the percentage increase in dividends over the four years, from $1.00 to $1.40, or 40 percent and dividing by the four years. The result is 10 percent a year growth.

The compound annual growth rate can be calculated using tables of the compound value of $1, or using a business calculator or computer software that has common mathematical functions. Using the table in Appendix E to this book, you take the number of years (4) and look to see the value of 1.40. This is between the 8 percent column (1.360) and the 9 percent column (1.412). Interpolating by taking the difference, .52, and dividing it into .12 equals approximately

25 percent, so the result is 9 percent minus .25 percent, or 8.75 percent. Note that this is quite a bit less than the 10 percent average dividend growth rate.

If a hand-held business calculator is used, enter the future value (1.40), the present value (1.00), the number of time periods (4), and press the CPT (compute) and %i function keys. You should come out with the same 8.75 percent compound annual growth rate or a number that's very close.

The *Value Line Investment Survey* performs these compound annual growth rate calculations for the companies on which they report. The numbers appear in a small box in the middle left of each company write-up. Among other financial data presented, *Value Line* includes the annual rates of change and change per share for earnings, dividends and cash flows for the previous five and ten-year periods. The investment service also offers estimates for two to three years into the future. Remember, though, these projections are only one service's opinion on what the future may hold. Other advisors may have different opinions.

PROBLEMS TO SOLVE

Company XYZ has had the following earnings had dividend history for the last ten years:

		EPS	Dividends
Begin Year	1	$2.35	$1.20
End Year	1	2.50	1.25
	2	2.65	1.32
	3	2.40	1.32
	4	2.70	1.35
	5	2.90	1.45
	6	3.00	1.50
	7	3.20	1.60
	8	3.50	1.75
	9	3.75	1.90
	10	4.00	2.00

1. What is the compound annual growth rate for the dividend over the ten-year period? For the most recent five years? Three years?

2. Is the annual percent increase in dividends accelerating or decelerating?

3. Has the payout ratio changed during the ten-year period?

4. Based on a dividend growth rate of 7 percent and a discount rate of 12 percent, what is the theoretical value of the stock based on the current dividend?

See Appendix A for solutions.

Chapter Four

SELECTING HIGH-YIELD STOCKS

How can you determine whether to invest in a particular high-yield stock? You need to ask two questions. First, is the company easily able to meet current dividend payments? Second, does it have the financial strength to increase dividends on a regular basis? The answer to these questions lies in the company's cash flow statements.

CASH FLOW ANALYSIS

Depending on the industry, cash flow can be as important as, or even more significant than, reported earnings. The amount of cash generated from operations is a key measure of a company's health. Because cash flow numbers can't be altered, they're a true indication of the quality of a company's earnings.

High-yield investors should learn the ABC's of cash flow analysis because cash flow is crucial to a corporation's ability (or inability) to maintain and increase the dividend. Good cash flows give a company tremendous financial flexibility. With recent tax law changes lowering corporate and individual tax rates, as well as eliminating the preferential treatment for capital gains, many companies will be looking to increase shareholder dividends; those with strong cash flows can do it more easily.

A number of earnings-related factors may make a company appear financially stronger or weaker than it really is. One-time capital gains, inventory revaluations, or write offs of money-losing businesses can distort reported earnings without affecting cash flow. Management may use these nonrecurring items to manipulate earnings. The financial community places tremendous pressure on them to show favorable year-to-year or quarter-to-quarter earnings comparisons. While reported earnings can be managed, cash flows cannot.

Cash flows can be calculated from the information contained in a company's "statement of cash flows" (formerly called "changes in financial position"). This data summarizes the corporation's sources and uses of funds for a particular time period. It appears after the income statement and balance sheet in a public company's annual report and quarterly reports. Using it, you can determine where corporate funds have come from, and where they've gone during a fixed period of time (quarter, six months, or year).

The statement of cash flow presents information on the operating, investing, and financing activities of the company. When the three sources and uses of cash are added together, the net result is the increase or decrease in the company's cash position. A typical cash flow statement appears on page 53.

In Exhibit 1, ABC Company increased its cash position by $13.5 million, most of which was generated from operating activities. Net income, depreciation, deferred taxes, a decrease in working capital, and the issuance of long-term debt played important roles in this increase. The major cash expenditures were for additions to plant and equipment and dividend payments on the common stock.

Most of the items appearing in the statement of cash flow are self-explanatory. The non-cash items added to net income in the cash flow from the operating activities portion of the statement are somewhat more complicated. These items include depreciation, amortization, deferred taxes, write-offs of investments, and other expenditures where no actual cash outlay is involved. It's important to know what these items are and how they relate to a company's income statement and balance sheet. Depreciation, usually the

Exhibit 1
Statement of Cash Flow
(ABC Company)

Cash Flows from Operating Activities	
Net income	$10,000,000
Add expenses not requiring outlay of working capital	
Depreciation	3,000,000
Deferred federal income tax	1,000,000
Decrease (increase) in working capital	7,000,000
Net cash provided by operating activities	$21,000,000
Cash Flows from Investing Activities	
Proceeds from retirement of equipment	$ 500,000
Purchase of property and equipment	(6,000,000)
Net cash used by investing activities	($5,500,000)
Cash Flows from Financing Activities	
Issuance of long-term debt	$ 6,000,000
Repayment of long-term debt	(1,000,000)
Retirement of preferred stock	(2,000,000)
Dividends on common stock	(5,000,000)
Net cash provided (used) by financing activities	($2,000,000)
Net Increase (Decrease) in Cash and Temporary Investments	$13,500,000

largest non-cash charge appearing in the income statement, is discussed below. A complete explanation of each of the other accounting items is included in the glossary in Appendix B of this book.

Depreciation is an accounting technique for writing down the value of assets over their useful lives on the assumption that plant and equipment eventually wear out and become obsolete after a period of time. Depreciation is a bookkeeping entry which shows how capital is consumed in the process of producing goods and services. It distributes the cost of an asset in a systematic and rational manner.

Annual depreciation is that portion of the total charge to earnings that is allocated to the particular accounting year in question. The depreciation expense is not cash set aside in a fund to cover the eventual replacement of the asset. Rather, it's a non-cash charge against reported earnings that reduces reported net income but has no impact on cash flow.

Many industries with heavy depreciation charges have cash flows double or triple their per share earnings. Capital intensive industries constantly invest in new plant and equipment. For them, depreciation is a very real expense similar to a cash charge because plant and equipment are actually wasting due to wear, tear, and obsolescence. Fixed assets must eventually be replaced using hard-earned cash. High-tech companies may face rapid technological change. Heavy expenditures for plant and equipment reduce financial resources available for other purposes, including payment of shareholder dividends.

For other businesses, depreciation is truly a non-cash charge. Prime examples are the cable TV and broadcasting industries, where property, equipment, and franchise costs may be depreciated over five years. The actual wear and tear on the system is a lot less. In fact, analysts value cable TV systems on a multiple of cash flow, rather than on reported earnings. The same goes for the broadcasting industry, where operating licenses are bought and depreciated, yet no actual obsolescence takes place.

Real estate investments are another example of depreciable assets that really don't depreciate. Although some physical depreciation takes place through wear and tear on the property, properly maintained real estate appreciates in value rather than depreciates. Because of this phenomenon, the common shares of real estate investment trusts sell on cash flows before depreciation rather than on reported earnings after depreciation charges.

Traditional cash flow analyses performed by Wall Street professionals use per share cash flow calculations. They take the net earnings and non-cash charges, add them together, and divide the result by the number of shares outstanding. In the statement of cash flows for the ABC Company which appears in Exhibit 1, assuming there were 5 million shares outstanding, the cash flow per share would be $2.80. This is derived by adding together net income ($10 million), depreciation ($3 million) and deferred taxes ($1 million) for a total of $14 million in earnings and non-cash charges. Therefore, cash flow per share is 40 percent higher than per share earnings of $2.00.

FREE CASH FLOW

A corillary to cash flow analysis is ''free cash flow'' analysis. The concept is to come up with a dollar figure for funds available for cash dividends after the company makes certain obligatory asset expenditures to maintain a competitive position within its industry, as well as honor its financial obligations. These mandated outlays include additions to working capital, investments in new plant and equipment, and debt service requirements. Remaining free cash flow can be used for dividend payments or other corporate purposes.

Discretionary cash flow is money left over after dividend payments are made. The company's survival is not dependent on these funds. Management may use them to increase dividends, make special share repurchases, prepay debt or make an acquisition or two.

Using the same statement of cash flow presented earlier, free cash flow and discretionary cash flow for the ABC Company are shown in Exhibit 2 on page 56. Applying ratio analysis, one can calculate the number of times the common stock dividends are covered by free cash flow. The higher this is, the greater the probability the company will increase the dividend in the near future. And the less likely the dividend will ever be cut. With respect to the ABC Company, free cash flow is more than twice the dividends, which is considered excellent dividend coverage.

Exhibit 2
Free Cash Flow
(ABC Company)

Cash flows from operating activities	
Net income and non cash items	$14,000,000
Decrease (increase) in working capital	7,000,000
Total Cash Flow	21,000,000
Required payments	
Debt service requirements	(1,000,000)
Capital expenditures	(6,000,000)
Total Payments	(7,000,000)
Free cash flow	$14,000,000
Less: Cash dividends	5,000,000
Discretionary cash flow	$9,000,000

Company boards of directors analyze corporate cash flows and the sources and uses of funds statements, current as well as projected, before determining dividend payments. With cash flows increasing, or capital spending requirements diminishing, dividends are most likely to be increased. When the opposite is true, dividends will remain flat or experience only token increases. As a potential high-yield stock investor, you should analyze corporate cash flow statements in the same way to anticipate future dividend actions by the board of directors. Note that an in-depth analysis of cash flows requires looking at the trends over several years.

As a company matures, it normally will generate larger discretionary cash flows. With sales slowing down, capital expenditure requirements are less and working capital needs don't increase as rapidly as they did during the growth years. The company can afford to pay out a higher percentage of earnings to shareholders. Slower growth

Exhibit 3
Dividend History of Growth Company

Year	Earnings	Dividends	Payout Ratio	Percent Increase
1	$ .75	$.03	4%	-
2	.90	.05	6	67%
3	1.10	.08	7	60
4	1.30	.10	8	25
5	1.55	.14	9	40

means lower share prices relative to earnings. This, coupled with larger dividends, mean higher yields for investors.

Cash flow analysis is almost irrelevant for growth companies because they're always spending more cash than they're generating. Earnings increase at a rapid pace, not only through the investment of internally-generated funds, but from external financing as well. Dividend payments represent only token distributions to shareholders to give them a sense of participation in company earnings.

With low payout ratios, however, growth companies can raise their dividends often and show shareholders large percentage increases. Exhibit 3 is a typical case. The payout ratio starts out small at 4 percent, but through large percentage increases in the dividend over a period of four years, the dividend rises by 350 percent from $.03 to $.14, and the payout ratio jumps to 9 percent.

A GROWING STREAM OF DIVIDENDS

In selecting a high-yield stock for your portfolio, you want to look at stocks with certain characteristics — a yield significantly greater than the market average, a dividend that's rising at least in line with the average of all companies, consistent year-to-year dividend increases, and a payout ratio of less than 60 percent. A combination of all three should ensure excellent investment returns for the high-yield advocate.

As a starting point, screen out any stock which does not have a dividend yield at least 33 percent higher than the market average, as measured by the yield of the S&P 500. Ideally, the yield of your stock should be at least 50 percent above the average yield.

Calculate the compound dividend growth rate over the last five and ten-year periods. It should exceed the averages of other companies. As a benchmark, the dividends of the Standard & Poor's 500 Index grew at a 4.8 percent annual rate for the five years ended September 30, 1987, and 6.4 percent for the ten years ending that same date. A dividend that doubles in 10 years grows at 7.2 percent per year; one that doubles in 5 years increases at 15 percent per year.

Look for stocks that have increased their dividends in at least 8 of the last 10 years, or better yet, in each of the past 10 years. Some investors will automatically sell a stock if the dividend is not increased within a 12-month period on the theory that the only reason for owning a stock, as opposed to a bond, is that eventually the yield (based on purchase price), will surpass that of the bond.

Make sure the dividend payout ratio is at a reasonable level—no greater than 65 percent—unless the company is experiencing a temporary downturn in earnings. Very high payout ratios mean that only a small amount of profits is being plowed back into the business to fuel future earnings growth.

HIGH-YIELD STOCKS AS BOND SUBSTITUTES

Another way to select a high-yield stock is to compare the dividend yield of a high-yield stock with the returns available from bonds or fixed income securities. This is the bond substitute concept, where high-yield stocks are regarded as having characteristics similar to bonds.

One way of measuring the value of a hgh-yield stock is to calculate how long it will take for the stock yield to catch up with the bond yield. If a bond yields 9 percent, and the stock you're considering

Exhibit 4
Bond Substitute Matrix
(Assuming Bonds Yield 10 percent)

Dividend Yield (%)	Annual Dividend Growth Rate (%): 4	6	8	10	12	15
4	23	16	12	9	8	7
5	18	12	9	7	6	5
6	13	9	7	5	5	4
7	9	6	5	4	3	2
8	6	4	3	2	2	2

has a current yield of 6 percent, then the bond yield is 1.5 times the stock yield. You estimate that dividends and earnings are growing at 10 percent per year. Using the Compound Value of a $1 table, at 10 percent per year, it will take 4.25 years for the stock yield (based on current price) to equal the 9 percent bond yield.

If the bond yielded 10 percent, the stock yielded 5 percent, and the dividend was growing at 12 percent, then it would take slightly more than 6 years for the stock yield to match the bond yield. This is just about the maximum time horizon you should allow for the stock yield to catch up with the bond yield. However, if the dividend growth rate appears to be slowing in recent years, you will probably want a shorter time horizon by opting for a higher-yielding stock.

Exhibit 4 offers a quick study on the number of years it takes for the stock yield to match the bond yield, assuming bonds are yielding 10 percent. The figures in the chart are yearly approximations; many have been rounded off to the nearest years.

Here's an example of how the chart can be used. With bonds yielding 10 percent, you are considering the purchase of a stock with a dividend that's growing at 8 percent and a current yield of 6 percent. Reading down the 8 percent column and across the 6 percent row, it will take 7 years for the stock yield (based on its purchase price) to catch up with the bond's 10 percent yield. Although this may seem like a long time, it doesn't measure the stock's total return, which is the current return plus capital appreciation. Hopefully, the latter will occur as rising dividends impact favorably on the stock's price.

As you review Exhibit 4, notice the relationships. The faster the dividend growth rate and the higher the initial yield, the quicker the stock yield (based on purchase price) will equal the bond yield. In other words, the length of time gets shorter as you read down and to the right in the Bond Substitute Matrix.

Another way of comparing a high-yield stock to a bond is to look at the implied rate of return for the stock. This is the current yield plus the dividend growth rate. Using an earlier example, the stock with a 6 percent yield and a 10 percent dividend growth rate had an implied rate of return of 16 percent, or 7 percentage points higher than the 9 percent yield on the bond. You must ask yourself if this is enough of a difference to compensate for the added risk of owning the stock. Don't forget that the higher the dividend growth rate compared to the current yield, the higher the risk of the returns not being achieved.

As with any stock selection process, there are many ways of going about it. The high-yield stock investor should use several of the formulas and analyses presented in this book as cross-checks on one another before making a final purchase decision.

PROBLEMS TO SOLVE

PROBLEM #1

A company with a high-yield stock has the following statement of cash flows in its annual report. You want to determine how adequate the cash flow level is relative to dividend payments and other financial needs of the company. A total of 5 million shares are outstanding.

Cash flow from operating activities:	
Net income	$25,000,000
Add expenses not requiring outlay of working capital	
Depreciation	10,000,000
Amortization of goodwill	2,000,000
Deferred federal income tax	3,000,000
Net change in working capital	(3,000,000)
TOTAL	37,000,000
Cash flow from investing activities:	
Capital expenditures	(5,000,000)
Acquisitions	(15,000,000)
Sales of long-term assets	4,000,000
TOTAL	(16,000,000)
Cash flow from financing activities:	
Mandatory retirement of long-term debt	(7,000,000)
Dividends on common stock	(15,000,000)
Sale of treasury stock	5,000,000
TOTAL	(17,000,000)
Net increase in cash	$ 4,000,000

1. What is the net income and cash flow per share?

2. What were the two largest outlays for cash and how much went to each area?

3. How much free cash flow was generated? Does this suggest a growth company or a mature one? Why?

4. What was the discretionary cash flow and what was it used for?

5. How many times is the dividend covered by the cash provided from operating activities? The free cash flow?

PROBLEM #2

The interest rate level for long-term bonds is 10 percent. You are considering the purchase of a stock that yields 7 percent and has a growth rate of 8 percent. The answers to the questions below will help you make a final decision.

1. How long will it take for the dividend yield to equal the 10 percent bond yield?

2. How does this dividend growth rate compare with the average for other stocks, as measured by the S&P 500 for the last ten years (1978-1987)?

See Appendix A for solutions.

Chapter Five

BLUE CHIP STOCKS

OVERVIEW

In poker, blue chips are the poker chips with the highest value. Similarly, blue chip stocks, and the companies they represent, rank highest in terms of earnings and dividends over a long period of time. When investors think of blue chip stocks, they picture America's largest and best-known companies.

The blue chippers are mature companies with slowing growth rates, better than average dividend yields, and large capitalizations. These companies are also noted for their ability and willingness to pay dividends on their common stocks through thick and thin. Blue chip stocks are widely held by individual and institutional investors alike; they are often referred to as "widow and orphan" stocks because they're owned by a high concentration of conservative investors.

Blue chip stocks can be found in many industries, including papers, chemicals, auto manufacturers, steel companies, retailers, oil companies and food processors. Blue chip companies are industry leaders competing in established markets. Some are in more cyclical industries than others.

Blue chip stocks are often equated with the 30 stocks that make up the Dow-Jones Industrial Average. However, several hundred other stocks included in the S&P 500 also qualify by virtue of their being among the largest industrial companies in America. This represents a large pool of stocks with above-average yields.

Over the long term, sales and earnings growth rates of blue chip companies parallel the American economy, as measured by movements in the Gross National Product. Because of their large size, the earnings performance of blue chip stocks can't match that of the pure growth companies. The larger the company, the slower the percentage growth rate. Therefore, blue chip stocks sell at lower price-earnings ratios and closer to book value than growth stocks.

The dividend yields on blue chip stocks are generally higher than those of other companies. The yield on the DJIA, which is totally comprised of blue chip companies, is about 20 percent higher than that of the S&P 500. With slower growth, less internal investment opportunities, and reduced needs for retained earnings, blue chip companies have relatively high dividend payout ratios. In addition, many have consistent records of dividend increases, although at modest growth rates.

ANALYSIS OF INDIVIDUAL STOCKS

How does the high-yield investor select blue chip stocks for his portfolio? The wide variety of companies that qualify makes the problem of security analysis difficult, for the blue chip companies are in many different industries. You must possess the skills to analyze both the industry and the company before making an investment judgment. This takes time and expertise.

An easier approach is to look for a situation where the dividend yield on a blue chip stock is higher than normal for that particular stock because of a temporary decrease in share price, not a recent dividend increase. This phenomemon usually occurs when the stock is out of investment favor for one reason or another.

Here's an example of how this strategy works: The shares of Blue Chipper Company have a generous dividend yield of 4.5 percent, while the average yield for all stocks is 3 percent. It sells for $20 a share with a $.90 annual dividend. Blue Chipper stock usually trades at a price to produce a yield 50 percent above the yield of all stocks. For one reason or another, the price of the stock suddenly swoons to $15 and the yield moves up to 6 percent, 33 percent higher than normal and double the market yield. No enhancement of Blue Chipper's dividend occurred during this time.

Upon further investigation, it turns out the investment community just became aware of some negative news about Blue Chipper. Earnings won't be as high as expected. With a large number of sellers and few buyers, the price of the stock fell by 25 percent, driving up the yield. The dividend was not impacted, although the chances for a dividend hike in the near term were probably scuttled by the negative earnings expectations.

At this juncture, the high-yield investor moves in and purchases shares hoping for a stabilization of the yield and an eventual recovery of the stock price. Patient investors usually are rewarded with excellent total returns in these circumstances. And the high-yield investor is amply compensated with healthy dividend income while waiting for the turnaround.

Out-of-favor situations can be found if the high-yield investor tracks a blue chip's stock yield over time, relative to the market. This can be visually seen in Exhibit 1, which assumes the average yield for S&P 500 stocks stays the same.

Exhibit 1
"Out-of-Favor Blue Chip Stocks"

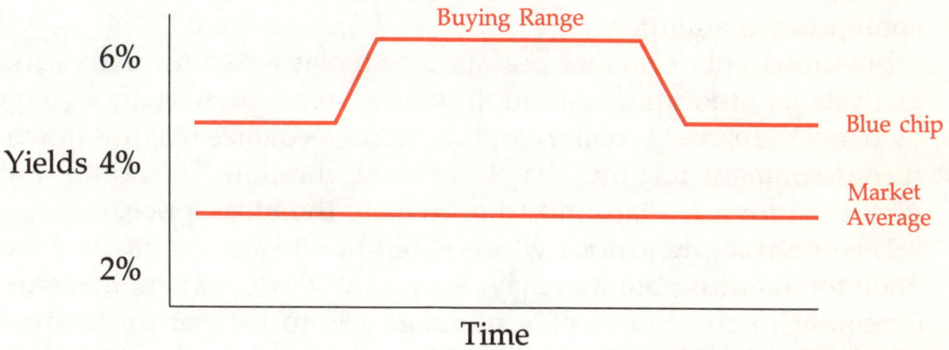

The time to buy is when the price has adjusted downward to reflect the higher yield. The investor must wait until all the negative news has been digested and the stock has moved down to a comfortable settling point and rested there for a while. Although buying at the low point is not easy to do in practice, the time to "bottom fish" often occurs after a steady stream of negative publicity has covered Wall Street.

An out-of-favor situation can arise for several reasons. It may be due to a recognition by investors of some sort of fundamental change taking place within the company or in the industry. Or it can be the fear that business adversity will occur in the near future due to forces or events outside the control of the company. In these circumstances, the price of the blue chip stock may never recover. High-yield investors should try to avoid these blue chip stocks.

Investment opportunities in out-of-favor stocks arise because of the market behavior of investors based on erroneous beliefs, wrong interpretation of events, overdone negative publicity, emotional reactions, or other factors which do not affect the fundamental financial position of the company. In the case of cyclical industries, investors don't care to own stocks of companies whose earnings are on the downward slope of the cycle. If a blue chip stock is out-of-favor for any of these reasons, then high-yield investors can profit from both more generous current yields and potential capital gains.

Wall Street has a great tendency to exaggerate both the positive and the negative when it comes to the stock market and the analysis of individual stocks. Analysts feel most comfortable projecting the current trend, even though it may be of short duration. With out-of-favor stocks, the negatives are in command of the investment community's attention.

Investment performance pressures also play a part. Investors and analysts pay too much attention to short-term performance (their own and the earnings of the corporation) to recognize that this downturn in company fortunes may be of short duration. They can't wait very long for a turnaround to rejuvenate the stock price.

If you can locate a stock which is temporarily out-of-favor, then good total return potential may be present for the patient investor. One way to check a stock's popularity is to look at the current dividend yield in relation to historical yield trends of the stock. You can get a feel for this from the Value Line's statistical charts on the companies it monitors which give the average annual yields for a fifteen-year historical period.

You can construct your own graph showing dividend yields over time for a particular stock. In order to develop a crude measure without too much effort, average the range of prices of a blue chip stock for each year and divide that average price by the cash dividend for that year. For example, if the yearly range was $20 to $28, then the average price would be $24. If the company paid a $1.20 dividend that year, the average yield was exactly 5 percent. Repeat the process for each of the past ten years and you will have an approximation of the historical dividend yields.

The Standard and Poors' Stock Reports (yellow tear sheets for New York Stock Exchange Stocks) are one source of historical stock price range information. Newspapers report the price range for the last 52 weeks in the stock tables. Historical quotes on a monthly basis for the preceding ten years may be obtained from the Dow-Jones News Retrieval computer system.

When the dividend yield goes significantly above prior levels, then consider it as a good time to buy the stock. Of course you first have to check out the reasons for the softness in the price of the stock. If you're satisfied the problems are temporary, then you have captured an above-average, high-yielding stock with potential for a capital gain bonus.

The risks of this investment approach to buying higher-yielding blue chip stocks is that their share prices may never recover as the fundamentals go from bad to worse. Earnings continue to slide, market share erodes, or the industry falls on its face for one reason or another. The stock keeps heading south as the dividend is cut and finally eliminated.

An interesting study was done, by an analyst at one of the regional brokerage firms, of the performance of the highest yielding stocks in the Dow-Jones averages. He studied these blue chip stocks for a period of sixteen years, and concluded that by holding the highest-yielding ten of the DJIA thirty stocks, the high-yield investor would capture much greater total returns than from investing in the Dow as a whole.

The methodology used was as follows: select the highest-yielding ten Dow stocks at the end of the year; hold them for exactly a year;

Exhibit 2

	10 HIGHEST-YIELDING DOW STOCKS			DOW JONES INDUSTRIAL AVERAGE		
YEAR	APPRECIATION	YIELD	TOTAL RETURN	APPRECIATION	YIELD	TOTAL RETURN
1972	– 1.5%	4.8%	+ 3.3%	–16.6%	3.2%	–14.4%
1973	– 9.7	6.8	– 2.9	–27.6	4.2	–23.4
1974	+48.1	10.8	+58.9	+38.3	6.1	+44.4
1975	+28.7	6.9	+35.6	+17.9	4.4	+22.3
1976	– 4.8	5.9	+ 1.1	–17.3	4.1	–13.2
1977	– 4.3	7.6	+ 3.3	– 3.1	5.5	+ 2.4
1978	+ 4.5	8.2	+12.7	+ 4.2	6.0	+10.2
1979	+18.7	8.6	+27.3	+14.9	6.1	+21.0
1980	– 1.7	8.0	+ 6.3	– 9.2	5.6	– 3.6
1981	+15.4	9.1	+24.5	+19.6	6.4	+26.0
1982	+33.0	8.1	+41.1	+20.3	5.2	+25.5
1983	+ 2.7	6.3	+ 9.0	+ 4.6	4.5	+ 9.0
1984	+16.6	6.7	+23.3	+22.8	5.0	+27.8
1985	+21.3	5.9	+27.2	+22.6	4.0	+26.6
1986	+ 0.9	5.7	+ 6.3	+ 2.3	3.5	+ 5.8
1987	+11.7	5.6	+17.3	+ 2.7	3.7	+ 6.4
SUMMARY	**+11.2%**	**7.2%**	**+18.4%**	**+ 6.0%**	**4.8%**	**+10.8%**

Source: John Slatter, Prescott, Ball & Turben Inc.

then adjust the portfolio so that the then ten highest-yielding Dow stocks were in the portfolio. Repeat the process at the end of each year. The results appear in the Exhibit 2.

During the sixteen-year period, the high yielders performed an average of 7.6 percentage points better than the Dow as a whole—18.4 percent compared to 10.8 percent—an impressive 70 percent difference. In only one year did a negative total return for the high yielders show up on the chart, and that was only –2.8 percent in the disastrous investment year of 1973 when the Dow itself had a negative return of –23.4 percent. The high-yielders failed to beat the total returns of the DJIA in just two of the sixteen years—1981 and 1984, years of very stong stock markets.

Most individual investors are probably not willing to apply this mechanical stock selection system. It's a no-brainer, it's boring, and although the returns are high, they're not exceptionally high. And by holding the highest-yielding DJIA stocks, they might have to put up with the occassional dividend cut or omission. Stock market investors would rather earn their returns the old fashioned way by making individual stock selections based on analytical research.

Perhaps the best rationale for the success of this approach (at least in hindsight) is that it leads investors to pick less popular stocks. If a blue chip industrial is out-of-favor, then its price will drop relative to other stocks. And the yield will rise putting it in the ten-stock selection category. But when the stock comes back in favor, or is not perceived in such a negative light, then the chances of it appreciating in value are good.

In the chart above, the average yield on the ten highest yielding Dow stocks was 7.2 percent or 50 percent higher than the 4.8 percent average yield for the DJII. Yet the capital appreciation for the high yielders was almost twice the rest of the Dow.

Although this is a rather simplistic high-yield blue chip investing strategy, you can get the same results by looking for stories on blue chip companies that are temporarily having a negative impact on price and are giving way to rising yields. You will have to brave the negative news and go for the yield. It's the old investment adage of buying on the bad news and selling on the good news. And if the company's financial situation doesn't turn around quickly, then you can collect those dividend checks while waiting for positive developments.

In the next several chapters we'll discuss what to look for when investing in specific industries where a majority of companies have common stocks which provide higher than average current yields.

PROBLEMS TO SOLVE

You have read some negative publicity about one of your favorite blue chip stocks. The stock price has dropped from \$60 per share to \$45 and you want to know whether now is the right time to buy. The historical dividend and stock price information follows:

Year	Price Range	Annual Dividend
1	$42-48	$2.25
2	40-50	2.30
3	43-56	2.50
4	43-59	2.60
5	33-46	2.75
6	50-59	2.80
7	48-58	2.80
8	46-57	2.90
9	58-67	3.10
10	57-70	3.25

1. Calculate the average yields for each of the ten years.

2. What year was a good one to buy the stock based on the dividend yield? What was the yield at that time and how much did it vary from prior years' averages?

3. Is now another good opportunity based on the $45 price of the stock and the current $3.25 dividend? What is the yield and how does it vary from average yields of the last few years and historical yields over the last ten years?

See Appendix A for solutions.

Chapter Six

PUBLIC UTILITY STOCKS

The high-yield stock investor has many stocks to chose from in the public utility area. These industries include electric utility companies, telephone companies, and natural gas distribution companies. These companies are regulated monopolies with established geographic franchises, stable earnings, high dividend payouts, and a fair amount of financial leverage. Deregulation is opening them up to greater competition, and at the same time, providing them with new business opportunities. In the rest of the chapter, the economics of each public utility industry is reviewed, along with pointers on what you should look for when analyzing individual stocks.

ELECTRIC UTILITY STOCKS

INDUSTRY OVERVIEW When investors think of high-yielding stocks, electric utility companies first come to mind. The yields on these stocks are often twice those of the S&P 400 Industrials, as a large percentage of earnings is paid out as dividends. Traditionally, electric utility stocks have been the most stable and conservative of all stocks, popular with the proverbial widows and orphans. Yet in recent years, some utilities have experienced financial difficulties and have had to cut their dividends.

Utility stocks with the highest yields naturally carry greater than normal investment risks. Investors perceive them as having unstable dividends. Utilities in this category may be in unfriendly regulatory environments, or have costly, uncompleted nuclear construction programs, or they simply have not been able to increase customer rates to recover construction cost overruns. In the past several years, 25 electric utility companies have cut or eliminated their dividends.

As a rule, utility companies with lower dividend yields operate in better regulatory environments, are non-nuclear providers, and have small construction programs. Their capital structure is solid, their dividends are secure, and it's more likely they'll be raised each year.

The stocks of electric utility companies are known to be especially sensitive to movements in interest rates. The reason for this is twofold. First, electric utilities are leveraged with large amounts of debt and preferred stock—usually about 60 percent of their capitalization—and they're always in the capital markets raising funds. As interest rates move up, their cost of capital increases and profits decrease. Second, because electric utility stocks are viewed by investors as bond substitutes, their yields move in concert with long-term bond yields.

In the 1970s and the early 1980s the electric utility industry was plagued with a myriad of problems including the oil crisis and increased fuel costs, rising interest rates, long and costly construction cycles, and high inflation costs. Negative investor sentiment drove the prices of electric utility common stocks below book value. After these negative factors finally receded into the background, the stocks of most companies regained their popularity.

Because utility companies are natural monopolies that supply a necessary service to the public, they are subject to intense government regulation, the most important being the rates charged customers. Regulators try to achieve a balance between investor and consumer interests. A good regulatory climate is one in which the electric utility is allowed to earn a fair return on equity and is actually able to achieve that return.

Recently, allowed returns on equity have been moving downward, reflecting lower inflation, taxes, and interest costs. Several years ago, returns were high when electric utilities needed to compete effectively for capital with other available investments in the capital markets.

Electric utilities now face deregulation and increased competition. As a result, more options to operate efficiently are at their disposal. Excess power supplies may be sold to other utilities. Sale-leasebacks of plants to private investors can enhance capital structures. Aggressive pricing strategies may be used to lure new customers.

The growth in electric power usage is related to residential and industrial demand, which in turn is affected by population growth and economic growth. Overall demand increases at a 2–3 percent annual clip. Residential demand for electric power is steadier, whereas industrial demand is subject to swings in the economic cycle. If a utility is too dependent on one or two industries, then demand can drop if the industry experiences a downturn. In some areas of the country, electric sales also depend on weather conditions.

Many utilities have finished large construction programs and are experiencing improved cash flows. Management can do several things with these funds such as reduce debt, repurchase stock, increase dividends, or diversify. However, in some areas of the country, due to changing weather and economic growth factors, electric utilities are reaching peak loads sooner than anticipated. Forecasts of rising demand may create a need for another construction cycle.

Electric utilities use different sources of fuel for their generating capacity, mainly coal, oil, hydro, gas, and nuclear energy. The relative cost of these fuels impacts heavily on the prices charged to customers. Most can be passed on, but low electric rates are an important incentive to attract new industry into the service area.

The environment is fast becoming a great concern for certain electric utility companies which burn dirty fuels. Acid rain from coal is a potential problem for many midwestern utilities. Others may have to convert to cleaner burning fuels as the greenhouse effect (hotter weather from breaking down the ozone layer) becomes more of a political issue.

A large number of public utilities have formed holding companies to use surplus cash flow to invest in unregulated businesses with larger profit potential. Some electric utilities have diversified vertically into oil and gas exploration, or into the distribution of heating equipment and appliances. Others have gone further afield with mixed results. The risks and rewards are higher, but successful diversification into non-regulated businesses bodes well for electric company earnings and dividends.

ANALYSIS OF INDIVIDUAL ELECTRIC UTILITY STOCKS

REGULATION In analyzing electric utility stocks, you have to review the past actions of the public utility commission in the state (or states) in which an electric utility is located to determine how receptive the regulatory climate is for rate increases and other actions. This information is also available through investment advisory publications and brokerage firms which continually assess the regulatory environment in each state.

Federal legislation to deal with the acid rain problem is forthcoming. It will most heavily impact those electric utilities that rely on coal as a fuel. They will either be forced to spend more money on environmental cleanup equipment or switch fuels. You must try to find out how much this will cost the company and what economic incentives and financial subsidies will be available to help out.

NUCLEAR EXPOSURE Perhaps the most important factor in the analysis of individual utilities is their exposure to nuclear energy, particularly those companies that are still completing plants. The possibility of another Three Mile Island nuclear accident always looms on the horizon. Such an event could literally bankrupt an electric company. It would taint the stocks of all companies with similarly constructed nuclear plants because major safety compliance corrections would have to be performed.

Many utilities experienced cost overruns in building their nuclear plants. State regulatory commissions have been coming down on the side of the consumer when utilities ask for rate relief to help pay for the huge construction costs. Not allowing the inclusion of all costs in the rate base has impaired the cash flows of many utilities.

SUPPLY AND DEMAND The supply of electricity is important in terms of peak load capacity. If a public utility operates near its plant capacity, then it must buy power from others or build new plants. The latter alternative can be expensive. Many utilities are deciding to use independent suppliers of electric power so they don't have the construction risk of adding generating capacity. Look to see what the utility is doing in this regard. Is it a net supplier or user of electricity?

FREE CASH FLOWS Examine the statement of changes in financial position to find out how much free cash flow is being generated and where it is being spent. In this connection, you will want to review the electric utility's future construction needs to see what the trend in cash flows will be.

DIVERSIFICATION Look closely at the type of deregulated businesses into which an electric utility company has diversified. As many industry executives have discovered, it's much tougher competing in the free market. Is the utility starting up new businesses or acquiring profitable going concerns? How far afield is the new business from the power industry? Does the utility management have a successful track record outside the industry, as evidenced by good earnings growth trends from non-utility operations?

RATIOS The key financial ratio for electric utilities is return on equity (ROE). This is net income divided by shareholders' equity. State regulators typically set ROEs between 12 percent and 15 percent. The amount of assets included in the rate base is also very important, as investors in many electric utilities with nuclear construction programs have discovered.

For those utilities undergoing extensive construction programs, you want to look at how much interest expense is capitalized during construction. This may have a positive effect on earnings, a negative effect on cash flow, and serious consequences for the utility if the rate makers decide not to include all construction costs in the rate base.

Another important ratio is the debt-equity ratio. Utilities are always in the capital markets to pay for construction programs. Because a large portion of earnings are paid out as dividends, they have to raise both debt and equity. The higher the debt-equity ratio, the higher the probability the utility will have to sell new stock which could dilute earnings. Historically, typical capitalization ratios have been as follows:

Debt	50%
Preferred Stock	10
Common Stock	40
Total Capitalization	100%

You also need to look at book value in relation to market price. Will new shares issued dilute equity because they are sold at less than book value? This became a problem in the early 1980s when electric utility company stock prices were depressed in a high interest rate environment.

DIVIDEND ANALYSIS The main factors affecting electric utility dividends are regulatory rate decisions, the quality of earnings, and future construction programs. Earnings without strong cash flows do not portend dividend increases. The most important consideration is how the utility is treated by the regulatory authorities for rate relief, especially in connection with bringing new plants into its rate base. Construction projects demand funds and compete with dividend payments for uses of corporate cash.

The managements of utility companies are very concerned with dividends because they realize that many shareholders rely on their generous yields for income. Any cut in the dividend is indeed a serious matter. Sometimes it's a signal to regulators on how critical the need is for financial relief. Once the dividend has been cut or eliminated, the board of directors tries to restore it as quickly as possible.

Historically, the dividends of electric utility stocks have grown at 3-4 percent per year. Growth rates have been higher for those companies serving population growth areas which are not caught

Exhibit 1
Historical Yields of Utility Stocks Relative to S&P 500 Index

	Electric Cos.	S&P 500
1984	8.7%	4.6%
1985	7.3	3.8
1986	6.3	3.5
1987	7.3	3.7

up in nuclear plant construction cost overruns. Utilities with successful diversification programs may experience even higher dividend growth rates, although, in the beginning, the cash flow requirements of these new businesses may put a damper on dividend increases.

Electric utility companies have always paid out a large portion of earnings as dividends to shareholders. The payout ratio has ranged between 65 and 75 percent. Historical dividend yield comparisons with the S&P 500 are shown in Exhibit 1.

TELEPHONE STOCKS

INDUSTRY OVERVIEW Telephone company stocks have high yields, but they're not quite as high as electric utility stocks — about two percentage points less. The reason? Telephone stocks offer shareholders more opportunities for earnings and dividend growth than do those of the power companies. Investors are willing to sacrifice some current yield for better growth prospects.

Most companies in the telephone industry are financially strong and mature with solid cash flows. The territorial franchises provide them with a steady stream of earnings. With funding needs for construction programs declining, excess cash flow is being used to diversify into new business enterprises.

In 1984, the number of available telephone company stocks increased dramatically when AT&T was broken up into seven "Baby

Bell'' companies. These regional holding companies, along with a handful of independent non-Bell telephone companies, comprise the universe of telephone stocks that are appropriate for the high-yield investor.

Providing basic telephone service to households and businesses has been a non-glamorous business for many years. However, the industry is currently embarking on more exciting ventures such as data transmission, video conferencing, faxing of documents, the development of private networks, and connecting automatic teller machines with telephone systems. Reflecting this change, telephone companies are now known as ''telecommunications'' companies, a high-tech sounding description.

Regulatory reform is one of most significant developments affecting the telephone industry. The shift toward fewer regulatory constraints is moving inexorably forward. Many experts believe that the telephone business should be motivated to upgrade systems and provide more efficient service, with all benefits passed on to the public in the form of lower prices.

Some regulators may decide to discard rate of return restrictions and tie telephone company earnings to a specified pricing structure. Other regulators want to detariff competitive services and permit profit sharing above a certain level of return in exchange for a combination of rate cuts and lowered rates of returns. This may have negative short-term effects on profits, but should bode well for the industry in the long run. Clearly, the future of the industry is somewhat clouded by the various proposals for changing the way telephone companies are regulated.

With telephone deregulation has come diversification. Some independents have been diversifying away from their basic telephone service for a number of years. A few have been successful, while others have had mixed experiences. Telephone companies are expanding into long-distance networks, cellular, cable TV, radio paging, computer software, and telecommunications software, most of which are growing more rapidly than the basic telephone business.

Telephone stocks behave like bonds and are considered by many to be a bond substitute. Shares of the regional Bell companies are the most sensitive to interest rate movements. However, as telephone companies expand operations outside their traditional, highly-regulated business into more glamorous areas, the bond subsititute label is being discarded.

Because earnings of the telephone companies are relatively recession-resistent, they are considered defensive stocks. Telephone shares sell at a 20 to 30 percent discount the market averages, based on price-earnings ratios. Although they sell at twice book value, many analysts believe the shares trade at sharp discounts to the potential break-up value of the companies they represent.

ANALYSIS OF INDIVIDUAL TELEPHONE STOCKS

REGULATION In order to analyze the stocks of telephone companies, you must look at the regulatory environment at the federal and state levels. Federal government regulators determine what businesses and geographical areas the regional Bell companies can enter. State regulators set the return on equity figures and local phone company pricing. The allowed returns on equity have ranged from 12.5 to 14 percent; however, reduced tax rates and interest costs have kept returns at the lower end of the range.

As with electric utility companies, some states are more consumer-oriented than others and take a tough stand on phone company rate relief requests. If price cap regulation is substituted for return on equity regulation, then telephone franchises in certain states could realize a significant jump in profits if their managements can quickly respond to new incentive pricing structures.

DEMAND FACTORS The condition of the local economy, gains in the number of access lines and long distance calling volumes must be analyzed to determine growth patterns for a particular telephone company. The business cycle does not impact local telephone usage because telephones are considered a necessity-type service. A recession may hurt long distance calling volumes somewhat, but this is not a significant factor for local or regional companies.

DIVERSIFICATION You need to look at the percent of revenue derived from non-telephone businesses and the profitability of these activities. Breakdowns are provided in telephone company annual reports in the financial section known as "Business Segment Information." Look at the consistency of earnings from non-regulated businesses. You will also want to know how aggressive the telephone company is expanding outside the telephone business and what risks management is taking. Some diversification efforts have not been successful.

FINANCIAL LEVERAGE For most telephone companies, equity has increased from 55 to 60 percent of total capitalization. With expansion into non-regulated businesses, you need to look at a company's debt in relation to those businesses. For telephone operations, debt-equity ratios of 50-50 are acceptable. In other business areas, 25 percent is more appropriate. As diversification efforts increase, financial leverage should decrease to compensate for greater risks involved with ownership of deregulated businesses.

CASH FLOW For most telecommunications companies, cash needs for the core telephone business have diminished and free cash flow is rising. Excess cash flow is being used for acquisitions and debt reduction. Although reported earnings are not rising as fast as dividends, this is due to higher depreciation charges. Telephone companies try to inflate their assets because this is the basis of their allowed rate of return.

DIVIDEND ANALYSIS Current yields of the telephone stocks are in the 5 to 6 percent range—about 60 percent above the market. Dividend payout ratios for telephone companies average 60–70 percent of earnings and only 25 percent of cash flow. Dividends are growing at a rate of about 6 percent per year which is slightly less than the pace of earnings growth.

NATURAL GAS STOCKS

INDUSTRY OVERVIEW Companies in the natural gas industry provide high yields on their common stocks, typically twice the yield on the S&P 500. Dividends are relatively stable and have been increasing over the years. Shares of gas companies that have

Exhibit 2
Historical Yields of Telephone Companies Relative to the S&P 500

	Telephone Cos.	S&P 500
1984	7.7%	4.6%
1985	6.8	3.8
1986	5.5	3.5
1987	5.4	3.7

successfully diversified carry lower yields, reflecting better prospects for dividend and earnings growth from their non-regulated activities.

The outlook for the natural gas industry is good. It's a clean, cheap, and abundant fuel. Natural gas could gain popularity as domestic oil reserves are depleted. Increased use of gas may be a long-term solution to America's environmental and import-dependency problems of high consumption of oil and coal.

Two groups of gas companies make up the industry. The first are the pipeline companies, which take gas from producing gas fields and transport it to gas distribution companies or directly to industrial customers. The pipelines are fast becoming common carriers subject to more and more competition as the industry deregulates under open access, where for a fee, anyone can transport gas through their lines.

Distributors make up the other group of gas companies. Sometimes referred to as gas utilities, they take gas from the pipelines and deliver it through their own gas mains to the end customers, either residential or industrial. Gas distributors are characterized by their heavy capital expenditure programs and stable base of customers. Their stocks carry slightly higher yields than those of the pipeline companies.

Several gas companies are structured as holding companies which own both pipeline and distribution companies. Because they're integrated, they have more flexibility in purchasing and pricing gas for resale markets. As might be expected, their common stock dividend yields fall in between those of the pipelines and distributors.

Sales and earnings for both pipelines and distributors are affected by several factors. One is the weather - cold winters are good for gas industry sales, as more gas is used during that time for heating purposes. Weather also causes a seasonal earnings pattern, where earnings are highest in the winter and losses are incurred during the summer months.

Another important factor affecting gas company earnings is the price of oil. When it's low, oil competes with gas for not only new residential customers, but for commercial customers who can easily switch to the less expensive fuel. Crude oil pricing acts as a cap on gas prices.

A final factor impacting on gas company earnings is federal and state regulation. Interstate pipelines are regulated by the Federal Energy Regulatory Commission (FERC), whereas the states regulate gas distributors by allowing them a specific rate of return on their equity.

The industry is currently experiencing an excess supply of gas known as the "gas bubble." Annual demand has declined from 20 to 16 trillion cubic feet, while gas supplies have remained steady. This market condition has driven gas prices down to very low levels with negative consequences for gas company profitabilty. Low prices are particularly harmful to pipeline and distribution companies involved in gas drilling and producing activities.

On the other hand, depressed gas prices are making gas extremely competitive with alternate sources of energy, helping to drive up demand. It also causes users to increase consumption and decrease conservation efforts. On the horizon are new uses for gas which will also help the demand side — cogeneration, commercial gas cooking, natural gas vehicles, and the use of gas for environmental reasons. World governments may take seriously the fears of the harmful effects of fossil fuel on the earth's atmosphere. As a clean burning fuel, this should add to the demand for gas over the longer term.

With domestic exploration for gas at very low levels, production is not being replaced and the gas reserve base is deteriorating. Experts predict that this phenomenon, coupled with greater consumer demand, may cause the gas bubble to disappear in the early 1990s.

Thanks to deregulation efforts, the Federal Energy Regulatory Commission's gas policy is oriented toward free-market competition. This means open access to pipeline usage for both producers and industrial gas customers. Likewise, gas distributors can search for the cheapest possible gas because they're not locked into buying from only one pipeline.

Pipelines compete against one another as they transport gas purchased on the open market. Large industrial end-users are buying cheap gas directly from the producers on the spot market, rather than through long-term contracts with pipelines. They use pipelines solely as carriers and pay competitive fees based on the distances traveled, a marked change from the traditional role of the pipeline as a buyer and reseller of gas.

If gas prices rebound, then distributors will move away from purchases on the spot market and enter into contracts with pipelines. The volatility of spot prices and the uncertainties of supply availability may cause renewed interest in long-term contracts. This will provide greater stability to pipeline earnings. It should also enhance distributor margins as industrial gas users make purchases through them instead of buying directly from the gas fields.

Outlays for pipeline construction will continue to grow as distributors search for cheaper gas supplies to capture new customers. The FERC has indicated a desire to expand pipeline service into the northeastern and western parts of the United States. This will add to construction outlays for some companies. Capital expenditures of gas distribution companies rise with new housing; however, such growth is expected to be modest.

Many pipelines have what are called "take or pay" problems from contracts they entered into with producers in the days when gas shortages were the norm. They contracted to buy large quantities of gas at high prices to ensure adequate supplies to customers. When prices dropped, pipelines were stuck with still having to pay for gas which they couldn't sell at a profit.

The pipeline companies are trying to negotiate their way out of these take or pay contracts by offering lump sum payments to producers. The FERC, through Order 500, has indicated that pipelines can recover up to 50 percent of their settlement costs from customers as long as they weren't imprudently incurred in the first place. Some pipelines have not been able to recover all costs, and, as a result, are experiencing financial difficulties.

ANALYSIS OF INDIVIDUAL GAS COMPANY STOCKS

REGULATION The returns on equity of gas distributors have come down in recent years because of lower inflation, lower interest rates, and lower federal income taxes. Some states are more cooperative than others on rate increase requests. You can get a feel for this by examining past requests and the percent increases granted by the state regulators. For pipeline companies, you need to look closely at what the take or pay contract buyouts will mean to future cash flows and earnings.

As regulated monopolies, gas distributors operate in state-awarded franchise areas. Competition is developing in some geographical areas where pipelines and industrial customers are allowed to deal directly with each other, thus bypassing the distributor. Any such trends in a distributor's territory must be noted.

DIVERSIFICATION You want to know to what degree the company has diversified away from the gas business. Unregulated areas may provide higher rates of return on invested capital and higher operating margins (income divided by revenue) than the gas business, but may increase risks. You have to look at sales and earnings of outside businesses and how significant they are to the company's overall operations.

Several pipelines integrated backwards and bought into the oil and gas exploration and production industry. Some distributors are supplying propane gas in rural areas of their marketing area. Others are diversifying further afield through the acquisition of such businesses as savings and loan associations, commercial banks, drug stores, containerized ships, and sand mining companies.

SUPPLY FACTORS Distributors are motivated to provide their customers with the cheapest gas in order to compete effectively with other heating sources. You should determine how much of a distributor's throughput is from spot sales and how much is from regular sales, because the latter has higher profit margins. When prices firm, those companies with a large percentage of spot sales stand to benefit the most.

LEVERAGE As regulated monopolies with relatively steady revenue bases and fixed returns on capital, gas companies can take on a high level of debt. Most have a debt-equity ratio of between 40 and 60 percent. Gas companies raise funds in the capital market to finance construction programs for new pipelines and gas mains.

Strong cash flows from depreciation charges and deferred taxes provide the means for servicing the debt. Examine a gas company's debt-equity ratio and free cash flows to determine the amount of funds available for dividend payments and the likelihood of dividend increases in the near future.

DEMAND FACTORS Gas distributors typically experience a 1 to 3 percent annual increase in new customers. Anything above that is considered a plus. In this regard, new residential construction in a distributor's territory is an important economic indicator. Gas companies can usually connect 80 to 90 percent of new homes to their network.

You should be aware of what percentage of sales goes to each category of customers, as well as the growth of sales to the residential, commercial and industrial markets. If the economy contracts, this could hurt pipelines and distributors that depend on industrial customers for a large percentage of their sales. Look at the BTU (British Thermal Units) numbers, not the revenue figures because fluctuating gas prices will distort yearly comparisons.

DIVIDEND ANALYSIS Gas companies pay out 75 to 85 percent of their earnings as dividends, although the payout ratio for a handful of stocks is in the 50 to 60 percent range. It's the normal tradeoff between taking a higher current yield with low growth prospects or accepting a lower yield coupled with prospects of accelerating dividends in the future.

On average, gas company dividends have been growing at a 7 to 9 percent annual rate. For gas companies caught up in the industry's problems, dividend payments have been growing at a faster rate

Exhibit 3
Historical Yields of Gas Company Stocks Relative to the S&P 500

	Pipelines	Distributors	S&P 500
1984	6.2%	8.0%	4.6%
1985	6.0	7.2	3.8
1986	6.6	6.2	3.5
1987	5.0	6.0	3.7

than earnings. Although this can't go on forever, gas companies pride themselves on their dividend records. In a few cases, companies hit hard with settlements of take or pay contracts have had to cut dividends.

PROBLEMS TO SOLVE

You are interested in analyzing the stock of a natural gas distribution company as a possible high-yield investment. You want to look at certain statistics before making a final decision, particularly the sales mix, cash flow, and industry segment data.

Sales Mix (BTUs)

Year	1	2	3
Residential	90	95	100
Commercial	47	48	50
Industrial	38	37	40
	175	180	190

1. Why should an investor be concerned with sales mix statistics for a gas distribution company?

2. Calculate the percentage of industrial sales to total sales for each year and explain the trend.

3. Why should one look at BTU sales rather than dollar sales to each class of customer?

The same distribution company had the following statement of cash flow, expressed in millions of dollars.

Cash flow from operating activities	
Net income	$20
Depreciation	15
Deferred taxes	3
Change in working capital	(5)
Total	33
Cash flow from investing activities	
Capital expenditures	(22)
Cash flow from financing activities	
Issuance of long-term debt	20
Dividends paid	(15)
Total	5
Net increase in cash	$16

4. How much cash flow was generated from operations?

5. How much capital was raised to finance capital expenditures?

6. What was the dividend payout ratio?

7. What was the free cash flow? By how much did this cover the dividend payments?

Industry Segment Information
(millions)

	Year 1	Year 2	Year 3
Operating revenues			
Natural gas distribution	$370	$360	$320
Oil and gas production	15	10	14
Other diversified businesses	5	14	26
Totals	390	384	360
Operating income			
Natural gas distribution	10	12	14
Oil and gas production	4	2	3
Other diversified businesses	1	5	12
Totals	15	19	29

8. Is it better to focus on revenues or income to determine the extent and success of a gas company's diversification efforts? Why?

9. What were the operating margins for each segment of the company in each year?

10. What percentage of profits (operating income) came from non-gas distribution businesses in the most recent year. What was the trend over the three-year period?

See Appendix A for solutions.

Chapter Seven

FINANCIAL STOCKS

Financial industry stocks provide another category of stocks suitable for the high-yield investor. This grouping includes commercial banks, insurance companies, and real estate investment trusts. These industries are more cyclical than the public utility industries, but their stocks offer good dividend yields and capital appreciation possibilities if bought at the right time. Wall Street classifies them as financial stocks because a large portion of their earnings is derived from investments, loans, and rents.

COMMERCIAL BANK STOCKS

OVERVIEW All banks are not alike. Commercial banks should not be confused with savings and loan associations which have been experiencing well-publicized loan problems stemming from outright fraud, insider dealing, and a variety of other dubious lending endeavors. Although not without problems, the commercial banking industry has had an enviable record of forthright and upstanding business dealings.

Commercial banks can be divided into two categories—money center banks and regional banks. Money center banks are the big New York City, West Coast, and Chicago banks with multi-national lending activities. Regional banks are located in smaller cities and rural states. Their stocks generally have lower dividend yields than money center banks, yet their yields are still a good bit higher than those available from industrial company stocks.

Money center banks rely heavily on loans to large corporations, international lending activities, and trade financing for the bulk of their earnings. Often referred to as "wholesale" banks, their yields have been higher than normal in recent years because of weak share prices due to the uncertainty of third-world countries defaulting on their loans. If this occurs, then money center banks will face huge write-offs and must raise additional capital to replenish their lending base.

Regional banks, known as "retail" banks, make commercial loans to local, smaller companies in their marketing area. They also engage in real estate and consumer lending activities. Regionals depend to a large extent on local deposits for their lendable funds.

Much bank acquisition activity is taking place at the regional level as states pass legislation allowing interstate banking. Several regional banks have acquired banks in nearby states to create super-regional banks. Although the purchases initially dilute earnings, the overhead expense savings from consolidation usually increases profits in the long run. However, strong internal controls are a must when managing newly-acquired banks from a distant headquarters.

In weak economic times, the prices of bank stocks tend to outperform those of industrial stocks as their relative profit prospects are better. Conversely, in strong economies, investors pay less attention to banks and concentrate on the stocks of industrial companies with stronger earnings trends.

The condition of the local economy in which a regional bank operates is important for bank profitability. A healthy local economy will produce good loan demand from both industry and consumers. And bad debt experiences should be lower. Although the national economy may be prospering, certain economic sectors often lag the rest of the country. The depressed southwestern oil states and midwestern farmbelt states are prime examples of where regional banks got stuck with many sour loans.

Stocks of both money center and regional banks are sensitive to interest rate movements which impact future earnings. A perception still exists that because banks lend long and borrow short, lower, not higher interest rates are better for banks. As banks try to match their borrowings to their lending activities, the impact of interest rate movements on earnings should be less than it once was.

The key factor for bank earnings to increase (and for eventual dividend enhancement) is for loan portfolios and the interest income derived from them to grow. But the loans must be judiciously made to minimize bad debt losses. In recent years banks have placed more emphasis on the generation of non-interest income. This includes fee income from bank service charges, trust income, and securities processing. The objective is to offset the cyclicality of interest income.

ANALYSIS OF INDIVIDUAL BANK STOCKS

Ratio analysis is a key component of bank stock analysis. Fortunately, banks present detailed financial reviews in their annual reports. They include many of the important ratios discussed below, which saves the investor time in making tedious calculations. In order to compare one bank with another or with the industry averages, you can use Standard and Poor's Industry Surveys, or Value Line's industry write-ups.

PROFITABILITY MEASURES Several important ratios are used in analyzing the performance of banks. The first is return on assets—net income divided by average assets. The range for most banks is .5 to 1.5 percent. The second is return on common equity, which is net income divided by stockholders' equity. This ranges from 10 to 20 percent.

LENDING ACTIVITIES You should look at the type of loans the bank makes and how diversified they are. For example, real estate loans are considered more risky than loans to large commercial customers. The greater the diversity of loans by type, industry and geography, the less overall portfolio risk is present.

Does the bank lend in its own terrritory or do its loan officers wander into distant lands in quest of new business? Some banks lend outside the area they know best—their own back yard. This can be a dangerous practice. It certainly hurt the earnings of eastern banks that loaned funds to oil and gas companies in the southwest.

LOAN QUALITY You should look at the bank's loan-loss ratio. This gives you an idea of loan quality because it indicates how much of the bank's loan portfolio had to be written off. Also determine what percentage of a bank's loans are non-performing. This means loan payments are 90 days or more behind and the bank is not collecting interest. Banks sometimes become too aggressive in their quest for loan growth by increasing lending activity to less than viable creditors.

You should look to see how much of a bank's loans to lesser developed countries (LDC loans) have been written off. Are all of them written off or have 50 percent or less been downsized? If a low amount is shown, then there may be more bad loan news to come.

RELIANCE ON OTHER INCOME You want to check on what percent of the bank's income is derived from customer fees and other activities besides interest income. The more income generated from non-interest sources, the less reliance there is on strong loan demand for bank earnings growth. This is particularly important now that banks are expanding into other financial areas such as insurance sales, merchant banking, security underwriting, and stock brokerage.

BOOK VALUE You should relate the price of a bank's stock to its book value per share. This is of considerable interest to investors who think a bank might soon be acquired. Well-run banks located in states that have passed interstate banking laws often have the potential acquisition price reflected in their stock price. Banks have been purchased for as high as twice book value.

Book value may be much higher than share price if it is perceived that there are large bad debt write-offs to come. This is true with some money center banks, where such charges to earnings could possibly reduce book value back down to share price.

DIVIDEND ANALYSIS The main factors that affect bank dividends are the bank's asset quality and the growth of its loan and service income. If asset quality deteriorates, additional equity capital will have to be raised to replenish retained earnings. This also inhibits dividend increases, and in severe cases, may precipitate a dividend reduction.

Bank managements are quite sensitive to their dividend policy because stability of dividends is an indication of the strength of the bank. The perception of a strong bank is important to retention of customers, especially depositors. Very few commercial banks have cut their dividends, although several large ones have done so in recent years to protect their capital base.

Cash flow does not influence bank dividend rates as much as it does for industrial companies, because banks do not have a large depreciable asset base. Banks have small capital expenditure programs limited primarily to building branch offices and installing data processing equipment. The major non-cash charge to income is the provision for bad debt.

Historically, banks have paid out only 30 to 40 percent of earnings as dividends. Because their shares sell below the market's average price-earnings ratio, dividend yields of bank stocks are relatively high. Dividends have increased 7 to 8 percent per year for the average bank. Those with loan problems have slower dividend growth rates as they must concentrate on building up their capital base to expand their loan program.

Exhibit 1

Historical Yields of Commercial Bank Stocks Relative to S&P 500 Index

	Banks	S&P 500
1983	5.5%	4.3%
1984	5.4	4.6
1985	4.3	4.1
1986	3.5	3.4

PROBLEM #1 TO SOLVE

A regional commercial bank listed on the New York Stock Exchange has come to your attention as a possible investment because of its good current yield and dividend growth prospects. Before making a final decision on the merits of the bank stock as an investment, you need to compute certain ratios based on financial information appearing in the annual report.

Financial Statements for Problem

Income Statement (millions)

Interest Income	$500
Interest Expense	300
Net interest income	200
Provision for loan loss	25
Net interest income after loan loss	175
Other income	75
Total income	250
Noninterest expense	175
Income before taxes	75
Income taxes	25
Net income	$ 50
Average No. Shares	25,000,000
Earnings per share	$2.00
Dividends per share	$ .75
Share price	$15.00

Balance Sheet
(millions)

Assets		Liabilities	
Money market	$1,000	Deposits	$3,750
Loans		Federal funds	1,000
Commercial	2,000	Other	350
Real estate	500		
Consumer	1,300	Total	5,100
Foreign	50		
Total	3,850		
Other assets	600	Stockholder's Equity	350
	$5,450		$5,450

Earnings and Dividend History

Year	1	2	3	4	5
Earnings per Share	$1.50	1.75	1.60	1.80	2.00
Dividends	$ .54	.58	.62	.70	.75

1. Compute the following ratios:

   a. Return on assets

   b. Return on equity

   c. Non-interest income as a percent of net interest income

   d. Amount by which price exceeds book value or *vice versa*

   e. Percent of commercial loans to total loans

   f. Percent of loans written off as bad debt (loan losses)

2. Calculate the following:

   a. Current yield of common stock

   b. Annual compound growth rate of dividends

   c. Current payout ratio and its historical range

See Appendix A for solutions.

INSURANCE INDUSTRY STOCKS

INDUSTRY OVERVIEW The stocks of insurance companies, particularly the property/casualty and the multi-line insurers, are another group of high dividend payers. Their earnings fortunes are tied to what is referred to as the underwriting cycle of the insurance industry. Even though earnings fluctuate, the steady dividends from these stocks provide support for share prices during lean times.

Property/casualty insurance companies write fire, auto, liability, homeowners, worker's compensation and similar types of insurance for businesses and individuals. The multi-line insurance companies cover these same areas, but also write health and life insurance policies for groups and individuals.

The insurance industry is highly fragmented with literally hundreds of companies selling a multitude of products. This fosters intense competition among insurers. It's also very volume-growth oriented industry, where sales ranking is an important psychological factor for top management.

Insurance companies write insurance policies, collect premiums, establish reserves against losses (claims), and pay out claims to policyholders. They earn income from the insurance underwriting side of the business as well as from the investment of their cash reserves in bonds and money market instruments. Typically, the industry moves from a highly competitive posture with heavy price cutting in property/casualty insurance premium rates to a less competitive environment where price increases are high enough to cover claim losses.

The key to the underwriting profitability of the property/casualty insurance business is the combined ratio. This is comprised of the loss ratio (ratio of losses incurred to premiums earned) and the expense ratio (ratio of expenses incurred to premiums written). If the combined loss and expense ratio is over 100 percent, an insurance company is losing money on its underwriting business. If it's under 100 percent, then the underwriting side of the business is profitable. A combined ratio of 110 percent means that for every $1.00 in premiums taken in, losses and expenses total $1.10.

Overall insurance company profitability is determined from earnings on on its investment portfolio. Hopefully, in times of high interest rates portfolio earnings will be more than enough to cover underwriting losses. If these losses can be controlled through proper pricing, then investment earnings should produce generous profits.

Typically, at the height of the underwriting cycle, the combined ratio falls below 100 percent while insurance companies are increasing their rates. As the cycle peaks, the combined ratio begins to rise above 100 percent. Insurance companies are willing to cut prices (premiums) to generate new business and build up reserves, for they know they can invest them profitably. High interest rates tend to aggravate industry price cutting because they produce more investment income on insurance company reserves and allow for greater pricing flexibility.

The key to investor success in the insurance industry is the ability to correctly predict the length and severity of the down period of the insurance underwriting cycle. If price cutting is not as severe or extended over a long period of time as expected, stock prices will firm and sell at higher relative values. Profitable investing in insurance stocks is also a function of a willingness to wait patiently for the next up cycle while being satisfied with good dividend income in the interim.

A very weak underwriting cycle occured in the 1981–85 period when rampant price cutting took place. Hopefully, the industry has learned some lessons from this experience. Property/casualty companies are now placing quality ahead of quantity when writing policies. New business is more carefully sought after, while sales incentive systems have been modified to limit the writing of unprofitable business. And the prospect of reduced earnings on reserves has a mollifying effect on premium price cutting.

Insurance company stocks sell at a discount to the stock market, as measured by their price-earnings ratios and book value. Insurance shares have historically sold at 75 percent of the market multiple and 85 percent of the market's price to book value ratio. This reflects the cyclicality of earnings in this business. Perceived as defensive stocks with less sensitivity to business cycles, insurance company stocks perform best in tough economic times.

The Tax Reform Act of 1986 has required insurance companies to ante up more taxes to the U. S. Treasury. Traditionally, income tax rates of property/casualty companies have been very low, running between 10 and 15 percent. The new tax law is complicated, but essentially it means higher rates and a speed-up in tax collections, resulting in a reduction of insurance company cash flows.

High inflation rates adversely impact earnings for those property/casualty insurers heavily involved in automobile underwriting. Ditto with soaring litigation costs and bodily injury awards. Multi-line insurers are faced with rising health costs which have eroded profitability, despite huge premium increases.

In recent years, large jury awards and out of court settlements have had a deleterious effect on the property/liability insurance business. Insurance companies are regulated by the states, and must have certain rate increases approved by them. The public is clamoring for control on premiums which have skyrocketed for certain types of liability insurance. Many consumers believe that insurance companies are conspiring to fix rates and restrict coverage by refusing to insure them.

ANALYSIS OF INDIVIDUAL PROPERTY/CASUALTY INSURANCE STOCKS

BUSINESS LINES In analyzing individual stocks, you should look at the type of business the insurance company is in, whether it be property, health, auto, commercial, or some combination of these. In the old days, insurance companies used to do a little bit of everything. Now many are restructuring by switching territories and changing their lines of business. Check to see if the company is moving into new areas where the competition is less. See if they have discovered special niche areas which look promising.

RATIOS You should look at a company's additions to reserves to see how conservatively it sets aside funds for losses. Analyze how fast premiums are growing. Calculate the percent of losses to premiums earned, and percent of expenses to premiums written, to determine the underwriting ratio. Review the yearly fluctuations in underwriting ratios to observe trends.

DIVIDENDS Insurance company dividends have grown in the 5 to 7 percent annual range, with some increasing as much as 10 to 12 percent per year. Average yields are not much higher than the S&P 500, but several insurance company stocks sport yields twice that of the popular averages.

REAL ESTATE INVESTMENT TRUSTS

INDUSTRY OVERVIEW An almost ideal security for the portfolios of high-yield investors is the real estate investment trust (REIT). REITs offer diversification away from stocks and bonds, as well as an inflation hedge in periods of rising prices. Well-managed REITs have produced excellent results for patient shareholders over

Exhibit 2

Historical Yields of Insurance Company Stocks Relative to S&P 500

	Property/ Casualty	Multi-Line	S&P 500
1984	5.3%	5.5%	4.6%
1985	5.6	4.4	3.8
1986	3.9	3.0	3.5
1987	3.2	3.5	3.7

the years. In fact, since the early 1970s, total returns for equity REITs have outperformed both stocks and bonds.

With REITs, the trust advisors buy and manage properties, or make mortgage loans and distribute the cash flow to shareholders. They operate much the same as mutual funds—a pool of assets under professional management. Historically, REIT yields have averaged 1.5 times the yield of the S&P 500, but some are two to three times. Yields vary depending on the amount of leverage used and the type of properties the REIT owns.

REIT yields are high because no income taxes are paid at the trust level and at least 95 percent of earnings are paid out to shareholders. Income-producing real estate can be purchased at a seven to ten capitalization rate, which is the same as a 7 to 10 percent cash return on invested capital. REITs typically trade at a 10 to 25 percent discount to the appraised (market) value of the underlying real estate in their portfolios. This discount adds to the yields stockholders receive.

The industry has waged a long battle to overcome the negative investor image of REITs, which dates back the mid-1970s when the value of REIT assets plunged by over 50 percent and many investors suffered huge losses. The main problem was caused by unseasoned REITs making bad mortgage loans to construction companies in overbuilt markets. REITs have staged a comeback as investors attempt to diversify their portfolios through various asset allocation strategies.

In recent years, a steady stream of negative publicity about overbuilt markets, high vacancy rates and forclosures in some parts of the country has kept REIT share prices relatively low. A better equilibrium between supply and demand is expected since passage of the Tax Reform Act of 1986, which eliminated the tax incentives for new construction and forced real estate investors to concentrate on a project's economic merits. This should improve real estate returns. Mounting inflation pressures may be an added bonus.

Over 175 REITs are active participants in the real estate market, investing their shareholders' money in office buildings, apartment houses, shopping centers, mini-warehouses, and business parks. Some are equity REITs which own properties outright; others are mortgage REITs that lend money to property owners, using the property as collateral for the loan.

Recently, several REITs have been structured as finite real estate investment trusts. The trust advisors will liquidate all properties after a certain number of years, allowing shareholders to realize the full value of their holdings at that time, thus closing the discount that REIT shares trade at from the appraised value of their properties.

The big advantage with REIT ownership is that these securities give liquidity to real estate ownership—you can buy and sell REIT shares (technically called shares of beneficial interest) just like any other publicly-traded stock. This feature makes them particularly suitable for high-yield investors who want portfolio exposure to the real estate sector, but are reluctant to sacrifice liquidity. This doesn't mean you trade REITs for quick profits. High-yield investors looking to maximize returns should plan on holding REITs for at least a three to five-year period to protect against having to sell in weak stock markets or real estate markets.

Tax reform had no negative impact on real estate investment trusts because they never were considered vehicles to shelter income from taxes. REIT advisors always had to use lengthly depreciation schedules for their properties and never really used much leverage. Actually, tax reform has established a level playing field where REITs are just as attractive a vehicle as limited partnerships for the ownership of real estate.

The stock performance of REITs is based on the outlook for the real estate market. They do very well in an inflationary environment. REIT stock price action is also keyed into interest rates. As with utilities, REITs compete with bonds for high-yield investor dollars. Yields on REITs and fixed-income securities move in tandem, with REIT yields lagging. REITs which concentrate on mortgage financing naturally have higher sensitivity to interest rate movements. In addition, in a period of high interest rates, it's difficult for REITs to make new acquisitions without diluting earnings.

REITs are noted for their defensive qualities. During the 1987 stock market crash, REITs fared much better than most other industry groups. In that fateful third week of October, 1987, REIT stocks were off just 11.0 percent compared to the drop in the S&P 500 off 22.9 percent.

In the best of worlds, REIT dividends increase at a steady pace each year as the trust's advisors raise rents on existing real estate holdings, or as more properties are acquired at favorable cap rates relative to the REIT cost of capital. REIT managements tend to hold properties for the long term to maximize returns and avoid having to sell in weak real estate markets; they will sell them only when better opportunities for increased trust earnings present themselves. It's the high current yield plus future share price and dividend increases that make these worthwhile high-yield stock investments.

REIT earnings can grow through reinvestment of retained earnings not paid out (usually only a small amount), or from higher cash flows from existing properties. The trust advisor may also sell new shares to raise additional equity capital. The proceeds are then used to purchase more properties with or without leverage. The ability of the REIT management to buy attractively-priced real estate, returning high yields with low-cost blended capital (debt combined with equity), adds to a REIT's growth rate.

Financial leverage reduces cash flow available for dividends because of the necessity of servicing the debt. But if the properties are well-managed, then the dividend and share price should rise at a faster percentage pace than for non-leveraged REITs.

The yields on leveraged REITs are not as high as those for pure equity REITs. But the dividend should increase at a faster pace and the capital gains should be greater. Therefore, projected total returns are higher. This compensates investors for the inherent greater risk of the leveraged REIT, where fixed costs must be covered whether vacancies are up or down.

ANALYSIS OF INDIVIDUAL STOCKS The real estate market is highly fragmented with many property owners and many different properties spread over the United States. Most REITS specialize in certain types of properties or a specific geographical area where they have developed expertise in buying and managing real estate.

PORTFOLIO COMPOSITION Before committing funds, potential investors must look closely at the property portfolio of each REIT to get a flavor for its composition. Are the REIT properties located in a sound economic area? Is its portfolio balanced and diversified? Is the advisor investing in more risky real estate ventures, such as hotels or restaurants? You should look at vacancy rates in the area where a REIT is operating to see if they are declining or rising. Although a particular area may be in good economic shape with low unemployment, it may be overbuilt with an excess of apartments or office space on the market.

CASH FLOW A REIT's performance is measured by its cash flow, which is defined as operating income before depreciation and taxes, but after debt service (mortgage payments). The proper analytical measure for REIT valuation is its price-cash flow ratio rather than the price-earnings ratio. You should examine per share cash flow trends for a recent period. The reason for looking at per share figures is that the better-managed, expanding REITs will be issuing new shares of stock from time to time. This causes temporary dilution, but when invested in income producing property, will generate additional cash flows down the line.

Another approach to REIT valuation is to calculate the cap rate you are paying for real estate based on the REIT's share price. This can be done by dividing the REIT's operating income by the sum of all its outstanding debt and its market capitalization, which is simply the price of the REIT share times the number of shares outstanding. Therefore, a REIT that earned $5 million, had $25 million in debt and a stock market value of $25 million would be selling at a cap rate of 10 percent. If the market cap rate for direct investment in real estate was 8 percent, then the REIT shares would be selling at a 20 percent discount.

LEVERAGE Examining leverage used by a REIT gives you an idea of how much risk the REIT is bearing. As with operating companies, financial leverage for real estate investment trusts is mortgage debt divided by equity (capital stock plus retained earnings). A leveraged REIT may have a lower dividend yield, but with a strong real estate market and good REIT management, the dividends should be growing at a fast pace.

It is also important to take note of the structure of the REITs debt. Is it represented by long-term mortgages or short-term bank debt? Does the trust have borrowings with variable rates so cash flow will be negatively impacted by rising interest rates. Are any of its mortgages participating? Are any of them the zero-coupon type,

Exhibit 3
Historical Yields of REIT Shares Relative to S&P 500

	REIT	S&P 500
1984	9.1%	4.6%
1985	8.6	3.8
1986	8.2	3.5
1987	7.8	3.7

where the REIT does not pay interest until maturity? This enhances current cash flow, but will become a liability when the property is sold and the deferred interest must finally be paid.

DIVIDENDS In order to receive their tax exemption from earned income, REITs must pay out at least 95 percent of income to shareholders. Dividend growth rates range from 6 to 8 percent annually. It's important to match up cash flow with dividends to make sure the REIT's divdends are supported by adequate cash flows. Some newly formed REITs start out by paying a portion of dividends from reserves. This technique of paying high yields from the start is used for the purpose of attracting investors in the initital public offering, but may have a negative impact if cash flow doesn't eventually increase to cover the dividend.

Historical yields on REIT shares compared to the S&P 500 are set forth in Exhibit 3.

PROBLEM #2 TO SOLVE

You have found a REIT that specializes in shopping centers. Better yet, it owns and manages a center located near your home which appears to be doing quite well. The REIT has 5 million shares outstanding, the share price is $15, the dividend is $1.35, and the market cap rate for comparable real estate is 8.5 percent. With a 9 percent dividend yield, you believe this REIT may be a worthwhile high-yield stock to add to your portfolio.

The following are some annual report statistics you need to analyze before making a decision:

Income Statement

Rental income	$25,000,000
Expenses	10,000,000
Income from operations	15,000,000
Depreciation	5,000,000
Interest expense	8,000,000
Net income	$2,000,000

Balance Sheet

Assets

Real estate owned (at cost)	$150,000,000
Cash	3,000,000
Other assets	2,000,000
	$155,000,000

Liabilities

Mortgages payable	$85,000,000
Accounts payable	2,000,000
Shareholder equity	68,000,000
	$155,000,000

Before making a final stock purchase decision, you want to answer these questions:

1. What are the REIT's net earnings and cash flow per share? Which is a more important indicator of a REIT's financial health and why?

2. What is the price-cash flow multiple?

3. Is the market value of the stock greater or less than the book value?

4. What is the cap rate based on the share price? Is this higher or lower than market cap rate?

5. Based on the answers to the above questions, is this REIT a good buy? What other information is needed to complete the analysis?

See Appendix A for solutions.

Chapter Eight

COMPREHENSIVE PROBLEM

You have come across an interesting blue chip company whose stock is currently yielding 7 percent. It sells for $35 per share and pays a $2.50 dividend. The company's earnings and stock price have been weak in the past year. You wonder if this is an opportune time to buy. You have just received the most recent annual report and want to analyze the company's financial data to determine whether you should add this high-yielder to your portfolio.

You compile a ten-year financial composite of earnings and dividends per share, along with annual price ranges of the stock. All nonrecurring earnings items have been eliminated. This is presented on page 116.

	Year	Per Share Earnings	Per Share Dividends	Price Range
Begin Yr.	1	$2.65	$1.15	-
End Yr.	1	2.85	1.20	$22-28
	2	3.20	1.37	20-27
	3	3.50	1.55	22-30
	4	3.75	1.68	24-29
	5	4.25	1.85	26-34
	6	3.60	1.90	23-30
	7	4.00	2.00	30-35
	8	4.50	2.15	32-40
	9	4.70	2.35	38-47
	10	4.50	2.45	35-42

Using this information you want to perform the following analyses and answer these questions before making a final stock purchase decision.

1. Calculate the dividend payout ratio for each of the past ten years. Is it increasing or decreasing? What does this indicate?

2. What is the compound annual dividend growth rate for the ten-year period? The first five years? The second five years? What trend is evident?

3. Determine the fair market price of the stock using the dividend growth rate of the most recent five years as the basis for future dividend growth. Assume a one-year Treasury note yields 9 percent and the risk premium in this stock is 4 percent. Is the stock fairly priced?

4. Calculate the average yield for the stock during each of the ten years. Is any trend evident?

5. What year would have been a good time to buy the stock when it was out-of-favor and offered a higher than normal yield? Is now a good time to buy based on current yield?

6. If bonds are yielding 9.5 percent, how many years will it take for the dividend yield on the stock to equal the bond yield based on the last five years' growth rate?

You should also analyze the cash flow statements below to determine the security of the dividend and future dividend growth before making a buy decision.

Statement of Cash Flows
($ millions)

	Year 9	Year 10
Cash flows from operating activities:		
Net income	240	230
Depreciation	120	125
Deferred taxes	15	20
Decrease (increase) in working capital	(75)	10
Total	300	385
Cash flow from investing activities:		
Capital expenditures	(120)	(90)
Investments in unconsolidated subsidiaries	(35)	(25)
Sale of equipment	25	30
Total	(130)	(85)
Cash flows from financing activities:		
Repayments of interim borrowings	0	(25)
Dividends paid	(125)	(130)
Purchase of treasury stock	0	(25)
Total	(125)	(180)
Net increase (decrease) in cash	45	120

7. Is cash generated from operations increasing or decreasing? What is causing this?

8. What types of investing activities is the company undertaking? What is the trend?

9. Is the company doing any outside financing? Based on the investing and financing activities, does it look like the company is a growth or mature company?

10. How much free cash flow is the company generating in year 10?

11. By how much are the dividend payments covered by free cash flow in year 10? Does the dividend seem secure and likely to continue growing?

12. Overall, does this blue chip stock look like a good high-yield stock for investment? Explain.

See Appendix A for solutions.

Appendix A

SOLUTIONS TO PROBLEMS

CHAPTER 3 PROBLEM SOLUTIONS

1. Compound annual growth rates for dividends are calculated by using a hand-held business calculator and taking the present value of the first year dividend, the future value of the last year dividend, the number of years, and computing.

   Growth rate for ten-year period is:

   PV = $2.35
   FV = $4.00
   N = 10
   CPT %i = 5.46%

   Growth rate for the most recent five-year period is:

   PV = $2.90
   FV = $4.00
   N = 5
   CPT %i = 6.64%

Growth rate for the most recent three-year period is:

PV = \$3.20
FV = \$4.00
N = 3
CPT %i = 7.72%

2. The growth rate is accelerating because it is higher in the last few years (7.72 percent) than over the entire ten-year period (5.46 percent).

3. The payout ratio is calculated by dividing the dividend rate by the earnings. It has dropped slightly from 51 percent at the beginning of the ten-year period to 50 percent in the final year. When earnings were down in year 3, the payout ratio increased temporarily to 55 percent.

4. The theoretical value of the stock is \$40. In order to arrive at this answer, subtract the dividend growth rate (7 percent) from the discount rate (12 percent), and divide the difference (5 percent) into the \$2.00 dividend.

CHAPTER 4 PROBLEM SOLUTIONS

PROBLEM #1

1. Net income per share is \$5.00. This is calculated by dividing the 5 million shares outstanding into net earnings of \$25 million. Cash flow per share is \$8.00, arrived at by adding together net income, depreciation, amortization, and deferred taxes, which equal \$40 million, and dividing by the 5 million shares.

2. The largest outlays of cash were for acquisitions and dividends, \$15 million each.

3. Free cash flow of $25 million was generated, based on the following calculation:

Cash flow from operating activities		$37,000,000
Less:		
Capital exp.	5,000,000	
Debt retire.	7,000,000	12,000,000
		$25,000,000

This suggests a mature company because it is generating cash in excess of its needs to grow. Very little cash is being plowed back into capital expenditures. The increase in working capital is small. It appears that growth is coming from acquisitions of other companies.

4. Discretionary cash flow was $10 million.

Free cash flow	$25,000,000
Less: Dividends	15,000,000
	$10,000,000

It appears the bulk of these funds were used for acquisitions.

5. The dividend ($15 million) was covered by almost 2.5 times with cash flow from operations ($37 million). Free cash flow ($25 million) covered the dividend by 1.7 times.

PROBLEM #2

1. It will take 5 years for the dividend yield to equal the bond yield of 10 percent. This is read off the Bond Substitute Matrix on page 59 in the text by looking down the 8 percent growth rate column and across the 7 percent dividend yield row.

2. The 8 percent dividend growth rate for this stock compares very favorably with the historical S&P 500 dividend growth rate of 6.4 percent during a recent ten-year period.

CHAPTER 5 PROBLEM SOLUTIONS

1. Average yield is determined by using the price range for each year to calculate the average price, then dividing the dividend by the average price for the year. Average yields are as follows:

   Year 1 = 5.2%
   2 = 5.1
   3 = 5.1
   4 = 5.1
   5 = 7.0
   6 = 5.1
   7 = 5.3
   8 = 5.7
   9 = 5.0
   10 = 5.1

2. The best time to buy the stock was in year 5 when the dividend yield was 7 percent, or almost two percentage points higher than in previous and subsequent years. Purchasing the stock at the average price for that year of $39.50 would have also produced good capital gains in the following two years.

3. A $3.25 dividend on a $45 stock translates into a current yield of 7.2 percent. Again, this is very high by historical standards and may suggest another good buying opportunity.

CHAPTER 6 PROBLEM SOLUTIONS

1. Sales mix data gives the investor an indication of the trend in gas sales to different customer classes, and shows how much gas is sold to industrial customers, who are most sensitive to business cycle ups and downs.

2. Year 1 = 21.7%
   Year 2 = 20.6%
   Year 3 = 21.0%

Each year's percentage is computed by dividing total BTU sales by sales to each type of customer. The trend of sales to industrial customers appears to be flat to down.

3. BTU sales are a better indication because they are not affected by changes in gas prices, which can fluctuate widely from year to year.

4. Cash flow from operations (operating activities) was $33 million.

5. $20 million.

6. Dividend payout ratio was 75 percent. Divide dividends paid ($15 million) by net income ($20 million).

7. Free cash flow was $11 million, based on the following calculation:

Cash flow from operating activities	$33,000,000
Less: Capital exp.	22,000,000
	$11,000,000

Free cash flow does not cover the $15 million in dividend payments. This is typical of gas companies who have large construction programs and pay out a large percentage of earnings as dividends.

8. It's better to focus on income when examining the success or failure of a gas company's diversification program. The goal is to increase the percent of earnings, not revenues, from non-gas activities. The investor wants to focus on the profitability of the diversification moves and how it impacts the bottom line.

9. Operating margins are as follows:

Year	1	2	3
Distribution	2.7%	3.3%	4.4%
Production	26.7	20.0	21.4
Other	20.0	35.7	46.2

These are calculated by dividing operating income by revenues for each segment in each year. For example, in year 1, the distribution segment margin of 2.7 percent was derived by dividing $10 million by $370 million.

10. To calculate the percent of operating income coming from non-gas distribution activities, it's necessary to add together the income from the gas production and other diversified businesses. For year 3, the most recent year, 51.7 percent of income came from non-gas distribution sources, a very high percent. Each year was as follows:

    Year 1 = 33.3%
    Year 2 = 36.8
    Year 3 = 51.7

    The three year trend was up, indicating an extremely successful diversification program.

CHAPTER 7 PROBLEM SOLUTIONS

PROBLEM #1

1a. Return on assets = 0.92% ($50 million divided by $5,450 million).

b. Return on equity = 14.3% ($50 million divided by $350 million).

c. Non-interest income as percent of net interest income = 37.5% ($75 million divided by $200 million).

d. Book value equals $14 per share ($350 million equity divided by 25 million shares). This is 6.7 percent lower than the share price of $15.

e. Percent of commercial loans to total loans = 52.4%

f. Loan losses written off as percent of total loans = .65% ($25 million losses divided by $3,820 million).

2a. Current yield of common stock = 5% ($.75 divided by $15).

b. Dividend growth rate = 8.6%

PV = $.54
FV = $.75
N = 4 (number of time periods)
CPT %i = 8.6

c. Current payout ratio = 37.5% ($.75 divided by $2.00). Historical range is from 33.1 percent (year 2) to 38.9 percent (year 4). This is a relatively narrow range.

PROBLEM #2

1. Net earnings per share are $.40 ($2 million income divided by 5 million shares). Cash flow per share is $1.40 ($2 million income plus $5 million depreciation divided by 5 million shares).

2. Price-cash flow multiple is 10.7 ($15 per share divided by $1.40 cash flow).

3. Book value is $13.60 per share ($68 million divided by 5 million shares). This is less than $15 share price, but does not necessarily reflect market value of properties, only cost basis.

4. Cap rate is 9.4 percent ($15 million in operating income divided by $85 million in mortgage debt plus $75 million stock market capitalization). This is higher than the real estate market cap rate of 9 percent, so the investor is buying real estate cheaper through ownership of the REIT.

5. The stock appears to be a good buy, although it's not extremely cheap at this time. One must review the earnings and dividend growth rate trends over time for a more complete analysis.

CHAPTER 8 PROBLEM SOLUTIONS

1. Dividend payout ratio is the annual dividend divided by the annual earnings. Ratios are as follows:

   Year 1 = 42%
   2 = 43
   3 = 44
   4 = 45
   5 = 44
   6 = 53
   7 = 50
   8 = 48
   9 = 50
   10 = 54

   The payout ratio is in an increasing trend. This means that more earnings are paid out to shareholders and less is retained for future growth. It suggests a maturing company, a characteristic of many blue chip companies.

2. Compound annual growth rates for dividends are calculated by using a hand-held business calculator and taking the present value of the first year dividend, the future value of the last year dividend, the number of years, and computing.

   Growth rate for the ten-year period is:

   PV = $1.15
   FV = $2.45
   N = 10
   CPT %i = 7.85%

Growth rate for the first five-year period is:

PV = \$1.15
FV = \$1.85
N = 5
CPT %i = 9.98%

Growth rate for the second five-year period is:

PV = \$1.85
FV = \$2.45
N = 5
CPT %i = 5.77%

Dividend growth for this blue chip company has slowed down markedly from just under 10 percent in the first five years to 5.8 percent in the last five years, although the growth rate for all ten years has been excellent. The company experienced two years of down earnings in the second five-year period which undoubtedly impacted the size of dividend increases.

3. The theoretical value of the stock is \$33.89. In order to arrive at this answer, subtract the dividend growth rate (5.77 percent) for the most recent five years from the sum of the yield on the relatively riskless 9 percent Treasury note and the 4% risk premium (13% discount rate). Divide the difference (7.23%) into the \$2.45 dividend. At \$35 a share, the stock appears to be fairly priced based on the approximately \$34 theoretical value of the stream of future dividends.

4. Average yield is determined by using the price range for each year to calculate the average price, then dividing the dividend by the average price for the year. Average yields are as follows:

Year 1 = 4.8%
2 = 5.8
3 = 6.0
4 = 6.3

5 = 6.2
6 = 7.2
7 = 6.2
8 = 6.0
9 = 5.5
10 = 7.0

The yield trend appears to be up slightly with a relatively high recent yield because of the depressed stock price.

5. Year 6 would have been a good time to buy because the yield jumped over one percentage point to an all-time high of 7.2 percent. Now may be another good time to buy because the yield has risen 27.3 percent to 7 percent.

6. It will take 6+ years for the dividend yield to equal the bond yield of 9.5 percent. This is derived from the Bond Substitute Matrix in the text by looking down the 6 percent growth rate column and across the 7 percent dividend yield row. Because the 5.77 percent dividend growth rate for the last five years is slightly less than 6 percent, the number of years will be greater (in the neighborhood of .3 through interpolation) than the 6 years shown in the chart. The 6.3 years should be about the maximum time horizon allowed for the stock yield to catch up with the bond yield.

7. Cash generated from operating activities is increasing in year 10. Even though net income was down, the decrease in working capital was a positive contributor to cash flow, whereas in year 9 an increase in working capital needs had a negative impact on cash flow.

8. The blue chip company is making capital expenditures and investing in its subsidiary companies. The cash flow needs for both are down in year 10.

9. No outside financing took place in years 9 or 10. Capital expenditures are financed internally. It appears this is a fairly mature company with not a large need for external funds.

10. Free cash flow of $270 million was generated.

Cash flow from operating activities		$385,000,000
Less:		
Capital exp.	90,000,000	
Debt retire.	25,000,000	115,000,000
		$270,000,000

11. Dividends are covered by slightly more than twice (2.08 times) free cash flow. The dividend appears secure and will likely grow, albeit at a slower pace than ten years ago.

12. On balance, the stock of this blue chip company appears to be a worthwhile high-yield investment. The dividend yield of 7 percent is at the high end of its historic range. Dividends are growing at almost 6 percent per year and the cash flow coverage is excellent. Assuming that earnings rebound and the stock price recovers, this investment should provide good total return to the high-yield investor.

Appendix B

GLOSSARY

AMORTIZATION—Accounting for expenses as applicable rather than as paid, such as depreciation. Amortization of intangible assets is another non-cash charge. Companies may purchase good will, patents and trademarks as intangible assets. The cost is written down over a period of years as the value of the intangible asset may decline.

ASSETS—Everything a corporation owns or is owed to it.

BALANCE SHEET—A condensed financial statement showing the nature and amount of a company's assets, liabilities and capital on a given date.

BETA COEFFICIENT—Measures the extent to which the price on a given stock changes with movements in the stock market.

BLUE CHIP STOCK—Stock of a large capitalization company in a mature industry.

BOND SUBSTITUTE—A stock that has a high yield and whose price moves in concert with bond prices so that the yield adjusts to changes in interest rates. These stocks may be purchased in lieu of bonds with the expectation that the stock yield, through increasing dividends, will catch up with the yield on the bond, whose interest payments remain fixed.

BOOK VALUE—The accounting value of an asset. The book value of a share of common stock is equal to the net worth of the company divided by the number of shares of stock outstanding.

BUSINESS RISK—The basic risk inherent in a firm's operations.

CAPTITALIZATION—Total market value of the various securities issued by a corporation, including bonds, debentures, preferred stock and common stock.

CAPITALIZATION RATE—Also known as cap rate, this is the cash on cash return from an investment, usually real estate. It can also be expressed as the operating income before depreciation, interest and taxes divided by the purchase price.

CASH FLOW—Reported net income of a corporation plus amounts charged off for depreciation, depletion, amortization, extraordinary charges to reserves, all of which are bookkeeping deductions and are not paid out in actual dollars.

COMBINED LOSS RATIO—For insurance companies, it is the sum of the loss ratio (ratio of losses incurred to premiums earned) and expense ratio (ratio of expenses incurred to premiums written).

COMPOUNDING—The arithmetic process of determining the final value of a payment or series of payments when compound interest is applied.

CURRENT YIELD—The annual dividend divided by the market price of the stock.

DEBT-EQUITY RATIO— The amount of long-term debt divided by shareholders' equity. A measure of a company's leverage.

DEBT SERVICE—Refers to the payment required for interest and retirement of the principal amount of a debt.

DEFERRED TAXES—(This is a difficult concept to grasp for non-accountants.) They arise from the difference in depreciation rates used for financial reporting purposes and tax purposes. When a corporation uses higher depreciation rates for income taxes than for shareholder reporting purposes (e.g., accelerated versus straight-line), the resultant lower tax liability shows up on the income statement. Deferred taxes are a non-cash charge to the income statement which equalizes the two different depreciation methods. This is offset by an addition to deferred tax liability account on the balance sheet, which is paid down in later years when depreciation rates for tax purposes are lower than those for reporting purposes. It's a complicated concept, but the point is that deferred taxes are another non-cash item that is a component of cash flow.

DEPLETION—Natural resources, such as oil and gas, metals, and timber are depleting assets. An accounting practice consisting of charges against earnings based upon the amount of the asset taken out of the total reserves in the period for which accounting is made.

DEPRECIATION—Charges against earnings to write off the cost, less salvage value, of an asset over its estimated useful life.

DISCRETIONARY CASH FLOW—Funds left over after dividend payments for use as management sees fit.

DILUTION—The issuance of more equity (common shares) that reduces the earnings per share of existing shares. The additional shares do not produce additional profit in the short-term.

DISCOUNTING—The process of finding the present value of a series of future cash flows. It is the reverse of compounding.

DIVERSIFICATION—Spreading investments among different companies in different industries or different businesses to reduce risk.

DIVIDEND—The payment designed by the board of directors to be distributed pro rata among the shares outstanding.

DIVIDEND REINVESTMENT—A program allowing shareholders to purchase additional shares of stock with their dividend payments.

DIVIDEND YIELD—The ratio of the current dividend to the current price of a share of stock.

EQUITY—The net worth of a business, consisting of capital stock, capital surplus and earned surplus.

FINANCIAL LEVERAGE—The ratio of total debt to total assets.

FINANCIAL RISK— That portion of total corporate risk, over and above basic business risk, that results from using debt.

FREE CASH FLOW—Funds available for dividends after certain obligatory asset expenditures are made up by the company to remain competitive in its industry and to honor its financial obligations.

GROWTH RATE—Percentage amount by which earnings or dividends goes up in a year or period of years.

GROWTH STOCK—Stock of a company with a record of growth in earnings at a relatively rapid rate, usually 20 percent or more a year.

HIGH-YIELD STOCK—Stocks with cash dividend yields considerably above the average for all stocks.

INDUSTRY RISK—When an industry becomes unpopular as an investment, all stocks in the group react adversely.

INTANGIBLE ASSETS— Intangibles often arise when companies are purchased. The difference between the purchase price and the net assets acquired is recorded on the balance sheet as good will. Accounting rules dictate that the good will item must be amortized over a certain number of years.

INTEREST RATE RISK—Security prices move in concert with interest rate movements. If interest rates move up, then security price moves down.

INVESTMENT WRITE-OFFS—Non-recurring charges to earnings when an asset is sold at less than book value.

LEVERAGE—The effect on the per share earnings of the common stock of a company when large sums must be paid for bond interest or preferred stock dividends, or both, before common stock is entitled to share in earnings. Leverage is good for the common stock when earnings are good, but may work against the common when earnings are bad.

LIABILITIES—All the claims against a corporation.

LIQUIDITY—Refers to a corporation's cash position and its ability to meet maturing obligations.

MARKET DISCOUNT—Percent by which a stock sells below the market average, usually measured by the price-earnings ratio.

NET WORTH—The capital and shareholder surplus of a firm.

OPERATING INCOME—Income before depreciation and taxes. A measure of profitability for real estate businesses.

ORDINARY INCOME—Income from the normal operations of a firm.

PAYOUT RATIO—Percentage of earnings a company pays out to shareholders as cash dividends.

PORTFOLIO—Holdings of securities of an individual or institution.

PRESENT VALUE—The value today of a future payment, or stream of payments, discounted at the appropriate discount rate.

PRICE-CASH FLOW RATIO—The price of a share of stock divided by cash flow per share for a twelve-month period.

PRICE-EARNINGS RATIO—The price of a share of stock divided by earnings per share for a twelve-month period.

PUBLIC UTILITY—A regulated monopoly providing service in a franchised geographic area with stable earnings and low growth characteristics.

RATE OF RETURN—The earnings divided by amount invested. Often expressed as return on equity, where earnings are divided by stockholders' equity.

REIT— A real estate investment trust that invests shareholder funds in a variety of income producing real estate, mortgages or some combination.

RESERVES—An account established for future losses. These losses are charged to the reserve account when incurred.

RESTRUCTURING OF BUSINESS—The process of selling certain divisions or subsidiaries and consolidating others to streamline or eliminate unprofitable or marginally profitable businesses.

RETAINED EARNINGS— That portion of earnings retained by the business for investment and other internal budgeting purposes.

RETURN OF CAPITAL—The portion of a distribution which is sheltered by depreciation or depletion and is not subject to current taxation, but which reduces the owner's basis (cost) in the investment.

RETURN ON ASSETS—The ratio of earnings to total assets, often used as a measure of a bank's profitability.

RETURN ON EQUITY—The ratio of net income to shareholders' equity.

RISK—The probability that actual future returns will be below expected returns.

STANDARD AND POOR'S COMPOSITE STOCK INDEX— A market value weighted index of the performance of 500 stocks.

TOTAL RETURN — The change in the value of an investment assuming reinvestment of income. For common stocks, it equals current dividend return plus or minus capital appreciation or depreciation, expressed as an annual percent.

YIELD—Also known as return. The dividends paid by a company expressed as a percentage of the current price.

Appendix C

BIBLIOGRAPHY

Graham, Benjamin; Dodd, David L.; and Cottle, Sidney. *Security Analysis: Principles and Techniques,* 5th ed. (New York: McGraw-Hill, 1988).

Heerwagen, Peter D. *Investing for Total Return* (Chicago, IL: Probus Publishing Company, 1988).

Hirt, Geoffrey; Block, Stan; Jury, Fred. *The Investor's Desktop Portfolio Planner* (Chicago, IL: Probus Publishing Company, 1986).

Mayo, Herbert B. *Investments* (Chicago, IL: The Dryden Press, 1981).

Standard and Poor's Industry Surveys

Value Line Investment Survey

Weiss, Geraldine, *Dividends Don't Lie*

Woelfel, Charles J., *Financial Statement Analysis* (Chicago, IL: Probus Publishing Company, 1988).

Appendix D

DIVIDEND REINVESTMENT PLANS

Two types of dividend reinvestment plan (DRIP) are available to shareholders. With the first, participants' dividends are pooled and sent to a bank which uses the funds to make share purchases in the secondary market. The shares are then prorated among the shareholders' accounts according to the dividend purchasing power of each. Most persons will end up owning fractional shares. Because a large block of shares is purchased, the commissions are much lower than if each shareholder made separate purchases on his or her own. Although shareholders usually pay the commissions, in some cases the company picks up the tab.

Under the second type of DRIP the company issues new shares from its treasury. The share price is determined by the market price (or some average price) at the time the shares are issued. No commissions are charged. This is an easy way for a company to raise capital, as new shares are issued and the proceeds go into the company's coffers for working capital needs or building and equipment expenditures.

With either plan, shares must be held in the owner's name; securities held by a brokerage firm in "street" name will not qualify. Many companies require that DRIP participants own only one share of their stock; others have higher minimums such as 25 shares for plan eligibility. As a DRIP participant, you will receive quarterly shareowner statements similar to those sent out by mutual funds which tell you the amount of dividends received, the number of shares purchased (including fractional shares), and the total number of shares owned.

Enrollment in dividend reinvestment plans is voluntary and you can withdraw at any time. If an account is withdrawn, certificates for whole shares may be received by the participant, or the bank custodian may sell the shares and remit the proceeds to the participants. In either case, fractional shares will be sold upon termination.

The advantage of dividend reinvestment programs is that few brokerage firms want to deal with small investors and their small investment accounts. Their profit margins are low or nonexistent on small trades. On the other hand, the commission charges as a percent of the trade price are extremely high for the small investor. Drips bring this cost way down.

Another advantage is that the DRIP is a means of forced savings for the investor. Dividend proceeds are automatically invested in additional shares so you never see them. For psychological reasons, many investors have difficulty investing when the market is down. The automatic nature of the DRIP eliminates this problem and allows you to accumulate more shares when they are cheap.

In addition to savings on commissions and other fees, DRIPs allow you to dollar-cost average additional share purchases. More shares are purchased when the stock price is down; fewer are purchased when the stock is up. As additional shares are purchased and the dividend is raised, the high-yield investor has more dividend reinvestment power. This process keeps compounding within the dividend reinvestment plan.

As with any good deal, there are drawbacks. Although you are able to dollar average, you are plowing more funds back into the same investment. This limits diversification potential because the investor's eggs are in one basket. If the price of the stock drops below what was paid for it with reinvested dividends, then you may have ''lost'' all or part of those dividends.

A final problem is that with a DRIP, the dividend income received from a high-yield stock is similar to ''phantom'' income. Even though you don't receive the cash dividends to spend, you must pay taxes on them. And if you're lucky enough to buy the shares at a discount, the difference between the price you pay and the market price is also taxable in the year of purchase.

Appendix E

COMPOUND VALUE OF $1 TABLE

Period	1%	2%	3%	4%	5%	6%	7%	8%	9%	10%
1	1.0100	1.0200	1.0300	1.0400	1.0500	1.0600	1.0700	1.0800	1.0900	1.1000
2	1.0201	1.0404	1.0609	1.0816	1.1025	1.1236	1.1449	1.1664	1.1881	1.2100
3	1.0303	1.0612	1.0927	1.1249	1.1576	1.1910	1.2250	1.2597	1.2950	1.3310
4	1.0406	1.0824	1.1255	1.1699	1.2155	1.2625	1.3108	1.3605	1.4116	1.4641
5	1.0510	1.1041	1.1593	1.2167	1.2763	1.3382	1.4026	1.4693	1.5386	1.6105
6	1.0615	1.1262	1.1941	1.2653	1.3401	1.4185	1.5007	1.5869	1.6771	1.7716
7	1.0721	1.1487	1.2299	1.3159	1.4071	1.5036	1.6058	1.7138	1.8280	1.9487
8	1.0829	1.1717	1.2668	1.3686	1.4775	1.5938	1.7182	1.8509	1.9926	2.1436
9	1.0937	1.1951	1.3048	1.4233	1.5513	1.6895	1.8385	1.9990	2.1719	2.3579
10	1.1046	1.2190	1.3439	1.4802	1.6289	1.7908	1.9672	2.1589	2.3674	2.5937
11	1.1157	1.2434	1.3842	1.5395	1.7103	1.8983	2.1049	2.3316	2.5804	2.8531
12	1.1268	1.2682	1.4258	1.6010	1.7959	2.0122	2.2522	2.5182	2.8127	3.1384
13	1.1381	1.2936	1.4685	1.6651	1.8856	2.1329	2.4098	2.7196	3.0658	3.4523
14	1.1495	1.3195	1.5126	1.7317	1.9799	2.2609	2.5785	2.9372	3.3417	3.7975
15	1.1610	1.3459	1.5580	1.8009	2.0789	2.3966	2.7590	3.1722	3.6425	4.1772

Period	12%	14%	15%	16%	18%	20%	24%	28%	32%	36%
16	6.1304	8.1372	9.3576	10.748	14.129	18.488	31.242	51.923	84.953	136.96
17	6.8660	9.2765	10.761	12.467	16.672	22.186	38.740	66.461	112.13	186.27
18	7.6900	10.575	12.375	14.462	19.673	26.623	48.038	85.070	148.02	253.33
19	8.6128	12.055	14.231	16.776	23.214	31.948	59.567	108.89	195.39	344.53
20	9.6463	13.743	16.366	19.460	27.393	38.337	73.864	139.37	257.91	468.57
21	10.803	15.667	18.821	22.574	32.323	46.005	91.591	178.40	340.44	637.26
22	12.100	17.861	21.644	26.186	38.142	55.206	113.57	228.35	449.39	866.67
23	13.552	20.361	24.891	30.376	45.007	66.247	140.83	292.30	593.19	1178.6
24	15.178	23.212	28.625	35.236	53.108	79.496	174.63	374.14	783.02	1602.9
25	17.000	26.461	32.918	40.874	62.668	95.396	216.54	478.90	1033.5	2180.0
26	19.040	30.166	37.856	47.414	73.948	114.47	268.51	612.99	1364.3	2964.9
27	21.324	34.389	43.535	55.000	87.259	137.37	332.95	784.63	1800.9	4032.2
28	23.883	39.204	50.065	63.800	102.96	164.84	412.86	1004.3	2377.2	5483.8
29	26.749	44.693	57.575	74.008	121.50	197.81	511.95	1285.5	3137.9	7458.0
30	29.959	50.950	66.211	85.849	143.37	237.37	634.81	1645.5	4142.0	10143.
40	93.050	188.88	267.86	378.72	750.37	1469.7	5455.9	19426.	66520.	*
50	289.00	700.23	1083.6	1670.7	3927.3	9100.4	46890.	*	*	*
60	897.59	2595.9	4383.9	7370.1	20555.	56347.	*	*	*	*

*FVIF > 99,999

Period	1%	2%	3%	4%	5%	6%	7%	8%	9%	10%
16	1.1726	1.3728	1.6047	1.8730	2.1829	2.5404	2.9522	3.4259	3.9703	4.5950
17	1.1843	1.4002	1.6528	1.9479	2.2920	2.6928	3.1588	3.7000	4.3276	5.0545
18	1.1961	1.4282	1.7024	2.0258	2.4066	2.8543	3.3799	3.9960	4.7171	5.5599
19	1.2081	1.4568	1.7535	2.1068	2.5270	3.0256	3.6165	4.3157	5.1417	6.1159
20	1.2202	1.4859	1.8061	2.1911	2.6533	3.2071	3.8697	4.6610	5.6044	6.7275
21	1.2324	1.5157	1.8603	2.2788	2.7860	3.3996	4.1406	5.0338	6.1088	7.4002
22	1.2447	1.5460	1.9161	2.3699	2.9253	3.6035	4.4304	5.4365	6.6586	8.1403
23	1.2572	1.5769	1.9736	2.4647	3.0715	3.8197	4.7405	5.8715	7.2579	8.9543
24	1.2697	1.6084	2.0328	2.5633	3.2251	4.0489	5.0724	6.3412	7.9111	9.8497
25	1.2824	1.6406	2.0938	2.6658	3.3864	4.2919	5.4274	6.8485	8.6231	10.834
26	1.2953	1.6734	2.1566	2.7725	3.5557	4.5494	5.8074	7.3964	9.3992	11.918
27	1.3082	1.7069	2.2213	2.8834	3.7335	4.8223	6.2139	7.9881	10.245	13.110
28	1.3213	1.7410	2.2879	2.9987	3.9201	5.1117	6.6488	8.6271	11.167	14.421
29	1.3345	1.7758	2.3566	3.1187	4.1161	5.4184	7.1143	9.3173	12.172	15.863
30	1.3478	1.8114	2.4273	3.2434	4.3219	5.7435	7.6123	10.062	13.267	17.449
40	1.4889	2.2080	3.2620	4.8010	7.0400	10.285	14.974	21.724	31.409	45.259
50	1.6446	2.6916	4.3839	7.1067	11.467	18.420	29.457	46.901	74.357	117.39
60	1.8167	3.2810	5.8916	10.519	18.679	32.987	57.946	101.25	176.03	304.48

Period	12%	14%	15%	16%	18%	20%	24%	28%	32%	36%
1	1.1200	1.1400	1.1500	1.1600	1.1800	1.2000	1.2400	1.2800	1.3200	1.3600
2	1.2544	1.2996	1.3225	1.3456	1.3924	1.4400	1.5376	1.6384	1.7424	1.8496
3	1.4049	1.4815	1.5209	1.5609	1.6430	1.7280	1.9066	2.0972	2.3000	2.5155
4	1.5735	1.6890	1.7490	1.8106	1.9388	2.0736	2.3642	2.6844	3.0360	3.4210
5	1.7623	1.9254	2.0114	2.1003	2.2878	2.4883	2.9316	3.4360	4.0075	4.6526
6	1.9738	2.1950	2.3131	2.4364	2.6996	2.9860	3.6352	4.3980	5.2899	6.3275
7	2.2107	2.5023	2.6600	2.8262	3.1855	3.5832	4.5077	5.6295	6.9826	8.6054
8	2.4760	2.8526	3.0590	3.2784	3.7589	4.2998	5.5895	7.2058	9.2170	11.703
9	2.7731	3.2519	3.5179	3.8030	4.4355	5.1598	6.9310	9.2234	12.166	15.916
10	3.1058	3.7072	4.0456	4.4114	5.2338	6.1917	8.5944	11.805	16.059	21.646
11	3.4785	4.2262	4.6524	5.1173	6.1759	7.4301	10.657	15.111	21.198	29.439
12	3.8960	4.8179	5.3502	5.9360	7.2876	8.9161	13.214	19.342	27.982	40.037
13	4.3635	5.4924	6.1528	6.8858	8.5994	10.699	16.386	24.758	36.937	54.451
14	4.8871	6.2613	7.0757	7.9875	10.147	12.839	20.319	31.691	48.756	74.053
15	5.4736	7.1379	8.1371	9.2655	11.973	15.407	25.195	40.564	64.358	100.71

ABOUT THE AUTHOR

Peter D. Heerwagen, CFP, is the principal in Heerwagen Asset Management Company, an an investment advisory firm located in Winchester, Virginia. The firm manages investments for individuals and small pension plans. He uses the high-yield stock investment strategy as part of his portfolio management program.

Mr. Heerwagen is a graduate of Princeton University and has an MBA in Finance from New York University Graduate School of Business Administration. He has the Certified Financial Planner designation from the College of Financial Planning.

Mr. Heerwagen has been quoted in several national newspapers and magazines on investing matters. He has authored *Investing for Total Return* (1988, Probus Publishing), *Self-Directed IRAs for the Active Investor* (1986, Probus Publishing) and co-authored *The Dow-Jones Guide to No-Load Mutual Funds* (1986). He also teaches business courses at a community college.